The Rule of Law: A Very Short Introduction

VERY SHORT INTRODUCTIONS are for anyone wanting a stimulating and accessible way into a new subject. They are written by experts, and have been translated into more than 45 different languages.

The series began in 1995, and now covers a wide variety of topics in every discipline. The VSI library currently contains over 750 volumes—a Very Short Introduction to everything from Psychology and Philosophy of Science to American History and Relativity—and continues to grow in every subject area.

Very Short Introductions available now:

ABOLITIONISM Richard S. Newman
THE ABRAHAMIC RELIGIONS Charles L. Cohen
ACCOUNTING Christopher Nobes
ADDICTION Keith Humphreys
ADOLESCENCE Peter K. Smith
THEODOR W. ADORNO Andrew Bowie
ADVERTISING Winston Fletcher
AERIAL WARFARE Frank Ledwidge
AESTHETICS Bence Nanay
AFRICAN AMERICAN HISTORY Jonathan Scott Holloway
AFRICAN AMERICAN RELIGION Eddie S. Glaude Jr
AFRICAN HISTORY John Parker and Richard Rathbone
AFRICAN POLITICS Ian Taylor
AFRICAN RELIGIONS Jacob K. Olupona
AGEING Nancy A. Pachana
AGNOSTICISM Robin Le Poidevin
AGRICULTURE Paul Brassley and Richard Soffe
ALEXANDER THE GREAT Hugh Bowden
ALGEBRA Peter M. Higgins
AMERICAN BUSINESS HISTORY Walter A. Friedman
AMERICAN CULTURAL HISTORY Eric Avila
AMERICAN FOREIGN RELATIONS Andrew Preston
AMERICAN HISTORY Paul S. Boyer
AMERICAN IMMIGRATION David A. Gerber
AMERICAN INTELLECTUAL HISTORY Jennifer Ratner-Rosenhagen
THE AMERICAN JUDICIAL SYSTEM Charles L. Zelden
AMERICAN LEGAL HISTORY G. Edward White
AMERICAN MILITARY HISTORY Joseph T. Glatthaar
AMERICAN NAVAL HISTORY Craig L. Symonds
AMERICAN POETRY David Caplan
AMERICAN POLITICAL HISTORY Donald Critchlow
AMERICAN POLITICAL PARTIES AND ELECTIONS L. Sandy Maisel
AMERICAN POLITICS Richard M. Valelly
THE AMERICAN PRESIDENCY Charles O. Jones
THE AMERICAN REVOLUTION Robert J. Allison
AMERICAN SLAVERY Heather Andrea Williams
THE AMERICAN SOUTH Charles Reagan Wilson
THE AMERICAN WEST Stephen Aron
AMERICAN WOMEN'S HISTORY Susan Ware
AMPHIBIANS T. S. Kemp
ANAESTHESIA Aidan O'Donnell
ANALYTIC PHILOSOPHY Michael Beaney

ANARCHISM Alex Prichard
ANCIENT ASSYRIA Karen Radner
ANCIENT EGYPT Ian Shaw
ANCIENT EGYPTIAN ART AND ARCHITECTURE Christina Riggs
ANCIENT GREECE Paul Cartledge
ANCIENT GREEK AND ROMAN SCIENCE Liba Taub
THE ANCIENT NEAR EAST Amanda H. Podany
ANCIENT PHILOSOPHY Julia Annas
ANCIENT WARFARE Harry Sidebottom
ANGELS David Albert Jones
ANGLICANISM Mark Chapman
THE ANGLO-SAXON AGE John Blair
ANIMAL BEHAVIOUR Tristram D. Wyatt
THE ANIMAL KINGDOM Peter Holland
ANIMAL RIGHTS David DeGrazia
ANSELM Thomas Williams
THE ANTARCTIC Klaus Dodds
ANTHROPOCENE Erle C. Ellis
ANTISEMITISM Steven Beller
ANXIETY Daniel Freeman and Jason Freeman
THE APOCRYPHAL GOSPELS Paul Foster
APPLIED MATHEMATICS Alain Goriely
THOMAS AQUINAS Fergus Kerr
ARBITRATION Thomas Schultz and Thomas Grant
ARCHAEOLOGY Paul Bahn
ARCHITECTURE Andrew Ballantyne
THE ARCTIC Klaus Dodds and Jamie Woodward
HANNAH ARENDT Dana Villa
ARISTOCRACY William Doyle
ARISTOTLE Jonathan Barnes
ART HISTORY Dana Arnold
ART THEORY Cynthia Freeland
ARTIFICIAL INTELLIGENCE Margaret A. Boden
ASIAN AMERICAN HISTORY Madeline Y. Hsu
ASTROBIOLOGY David C. Catling
ASTROPHYSICS James Binney
ATHEISM Julian Baggini
THE ATMOSPHERE Paul I. Palmer
AUGUSTINE Henry Chadwick
JANE AUSTEN Tom Keymer
AUSTRALIA Kenneth Morgan
AUTHORITARIANISM James Loxton
AUTISM Uta Frith
AUTOBIOGRAPHY Laura Marcus
THE AVANT GARDE David Cottington
THE AZTECS Davíd Carrasco
BABYLONIA Trevor Bryce
BACTERIA Sebastian G. B. Amyes
BANKING John Goddard and John O. S. Wilson
BARTHES Jonathan Culler
THE BEATS David Sterritt
BEAUTY Roger Scruton
LUDWIG VAN BEETHOVEN Mark Evan Bonds
BEHAVIOURAL ECONOMICS Michelle Baddeley
BESTSELLERS John Sutherland
THE BIBLE John Riches
BIBLICAL ARCHAEOLOGY Eric H. Cline
BIG DATA Dawn E. Holmes
BIOCHEMISTRY Mark Lorch
BIODIVERSITY CONSERVATION David Macdonald
BIOGEOGRAPHY Mark V. Lomolino
BIOGRAPHY Hermione Lee
BIOMETRICS Michael Fairhurst
ELIZABETH BISHOP Jonathan F. S. Post
BLACK HOLES Katherine Blundell
BLASPHEMY Yvonne Sherwood
BLOOD Chris Cooper
THE BLUES Elijah Wald
THE BODY Chris Shilling
THE BOHEMIANS David Weir
NIELS BOHR J. L. Heilbron
THE BOOK OF COMMON PRAYER Brian Cummings
THE BOOK OF MORMON Terryl Givens
BORDERS Alexander C. Diener and Joshua Hagen
THE BRAIN Michael O'Shea
BRANDING Robert Jones
THE BRICS Andrew F. Cooper
BRITISH ARCHITECTURE Dana Arnold
BRITISH CINEMA Charles Barr

THE BRITISH CONSTITUTION Martin Loughlin
THE BRITISH EMPIRE Ashley Jackson
BRITISH POLITICS Tony Wright
BUDDHA Michael Carrithers
BUDDHISM Damien Keown
BUDDHIST ETHICS Damien Keown
BYZANTIUM Peter Sarris
CALVINISM Jon Balserak
ALBERT CAMUS Oliver Gloag
CANADA Donald Wright
CANCER Nicholas James
CAPITALISM James Fulcher
CATHOLICISM Gerald O'Collins
CAUSATION Stephen Mumford and Rani Lill Anjum
THE CELL Terence Allen and Graham Cowling
THE CELTS Barry Cunliffe
CHAOS Leonard Smith
GEOFFREY CHAUCER David Wallace
CHEMISTRY Peter Atkins
CHILD PSYCHOLOGY Usha Goswami
CHILDREN'S LITERATURE Kimberley Reynolds
CHINESE LITERATURE Sabina Knight
CHOICE THEORY Michael Allingham
CHRISTIAN ART Beth Williamson
CHRISTIAN ETHICS D. Stephen Long
CHRISTIANITY Linda Woodhead
CIRCADIAN RHYTHMS Russell Foster and Leon Kreitzman
CITIZENSHIP Richard Bellamy
CITY PLANNING Carl Abbott
CIVIL ENGINEERING David Muir Wood
THE CIVIL RIGHTS MOVEMENT Thomas C. Holt
CIVIL WARS Monica Duffy Toft
CLASSICAL LITERATURE William Allan
CLASSICAL MYTHOLOGY Helen Morales
CLASSICS Mary Beard and John Henderson
CLAUSEWITZ Michael Howard
CLIMATE Mark Maslin
CLIMATE CHANGE Mark Maslin
CLINICAL PSYCHOLOGY Susan Llewelyn and Katie Aafjes-van Doorn
COGNITIVE BEHAVIOURAL THERAPY Freda McManus
COGNITIVE NEUROSCIENCE Richard Passingham
THE COLD WAR Robert J. McMahon
COLONIAL AMERICA Alan Taylor
COLONIAL LATIN AMERICAN LITERATURE Rolena Adorno
COMBINATORICS Robin Wilson
COMEDY Matthew Bevis
COMMUNISM Leslie Holmes
COMPARATIVE LAW Sabrina Ragone and Guido Smorto
COMPARATIVE LITERATURE Ben Hutchinson
COMPETITION AND ANTITRUST LAW Ariel Ezrachi
COMPLEXITY John H. Holland
THE COMPUTER Darrel Ince
COMPUTER SCIENCE Subrata Dasgupta
CONCENTRATION CAMPS Dan Stone
CONDENSED MATTER PHYSICS Ross H. McKenzie
CONFUCIANISM Daniel K. Gardner
THE CONQUISTADORS Matthew Restall and Felipe Fernández-Armesto
CONSCIENCE Paul Strohm
CONSCIOUSNESS Susan Blackmore
CONTEMPORARY ART Julian Stallabrass
CONTEMPORARY FICTION Robert Eaglestone
CONTINENTAL PHILOSOPHY Simon Critchley
COPERNICUS Owen Gingerich
CORAL REEFS Charles Sheppard
CORPORATE SOCIAL RESPONSIBILITY Jeremy Moon
CORRUPTION Leslie Holmes
COSMOLOGY Peter Coles
COUNTRY MUSIC Richard Carlin
CREATIVITY Vlad Glăveanu
CRIME FICTION Richard Bradford
CRIMINAL JUSTICE Julian V. Roberts
CRIMINOLOGY Tim Newburn
CRITICAL THEORY Stephen Eric Bronner
THE CRUSADES Christopher Tyerman
CRYPTOGRAPHY Fred Piper and Sean Murphy
CRYSTALLOGRAPHY A. M. Glazer

THE CULTURAL REVOLUTION Richard Curt Kraus
DADA AND SURREALISM David Hopkins
DANTE Peter Hainsworth and David Robey
DARWIN Jonathan Howard
THE DEAD SEA SCROLLS Timothy H. Lim
DECADENCE David Weir
DECOLONIZATION Dane Kennedy
DEMENTIA Kathleen Taylor
DEMOCRACY Naomi Zack
DEMOGRAPHY Sarah Harper
DEPRESSION Jan Scott and Mary Jane Tacchi
DERRIDA Simon Glendinning
DESCARTES Tom Sorell
DESERTS Nick Middleton
DESIGN John Heskett
DEVELOPMENT Ian Goldin
DEVELOPMENTAL BIOLOGY Lewis Wolpert
THE DEVIL Darren Oldridge
DIASPORA Kevin Kenny
CHARLES DICKENS Jenny Hartley
DICTIONARIES Lynda Mugglestone
DINOSAURS David Norman
DIPLOMATIC HISTORY Joseph M. Siracusa
DOCUMENTARY FILM Patricia Aufderheide
DOSTOEVSKY Deborah Martinsen
DREAMING J. Allan Hobson
DRUGS Les Iversen
DRUIDS Barry Cunliffe
DYNASTY Jeroen Duindam
DYSLEXIA Margaret J. Snowling
EARLY MUSIC Thomas Forrest Kelly
THE EARTH Martin Redfern
EARTH SYSTEM SCIENCE Tim Lenton
ECOLOGY Jaboury Ghazoul
ECONOMICS Partha Dasgupta
EDUCATION Gary Thomas
EGYPTIAN MYTH Geraldine Pinch
EIGHTEENTH-CENTURY BRITAIN Paul Langford
ELECTIONS L. Sandy Maisel and Jennifer A. Yoder
THE ELEMENTS Philip Ball
EMOTION Dylan Evans
EMPIRE Stephen Howe
EMPLOYMENT LAW David Cabrelli
ENERGY SYSTEMS Nick Jenkins
ENGELS Terrell Carver
ENGINEERING David Blockley
THE ENGLISH LANGUAGE Simon Horobin
ENGLISH LITERATURE Jonathan Bate
THE ENLIGHTENMENT John Robertson
ENTREPRENEURSHIP Paul Westhead and Mike Wright
ENVIRONMENTAL ECONOMICS Stephen Smith
ENVIRONMENTAL ETHICS Robin Attfield
ENVIRONMENTAL LAW Elizabeth Fisher
ENVIRONMENTAL POLITICS Andrew Dobson
ENZYMES Paul Engel
THE EPIC Anthony Welch
EPICUREANISM Catherine Wilson
EPIDEMIOLOGY Rodolfo Saracci
ETHICS Simon Blackburn
ETHNOMUSICOLOGY Timothy Rice
THE ETRUSCANS Christopher Smith
EUGENICS Philippa Levine
THE EUROPEAN UNION Simon Usherwood and John Pinder
EUROPEAN UNION LAW Anthony Arnull
EVANGELICALISM John G. Stackhouse Jr.
EVIL Luke Russell
EVOLUTION Brian and Deborah Charlesworth
EXISTENTIALISM Thomas Flynn
EXPLORATION Stewart A. Weaver
EXTINCTION Paul B. Wignall
THE EYE Michael Land
FAIRY TALE Marina Warner
FAITH Roger Trigg
FAMILY LAW Jonathan Herring
MICHAEL FARADAY Frank A. J. L. James
FASCISM Kevin Passmore
FASHION Rebecca Arnold
FEDERALISM Mark J. Rozell and Clyde Wilcox

FEMINISM Margaret Walters
FEMINIST PHILOSOPHY Katharine Jenkins
FILM Michael Wood
FILM MUSIC Kathryn Kalinak
FILM NOIR James Naremore
FIRE Andrew C. Scott
THE FIRST WORLD WAR Michael Howard
FLUID MECHANICS Eric Lauga
FOLK MUSIC Mark Slobin
FOOD John Krebs
FORENSIC PSYCHOLOGY David Canter
FORENSIC SCIENCE Jim Fraser
FORESTS Jaboury Ghazoul
FOSSILS Keith Thomson
FOUCAULT Gary Gutting
THE FOUNDING FATHERS R. B. Bernstein
FRACTALS Kenneth Falconer
FREE SPEECH Nigel Warburton
FREE WILL Thomas Pink
FREEMASONRY Andreas Önnerfors
FRENCH CINEMA Dudley Andrew
FRENCH LITERATURE John D. Lyons
FRENCH PHILOSOPHY Stephen Gaukroger and Knox Peden
THE FRENCH REVOLUTION William Doyle
FREUD Anthony Storr
FUNDAMENTALISM Malise Ruthven
FUNGI Nicholas P. Money
THE FUTURE Jennifer M. Gidley
GALAXIES John Gribbin
GALILEO Stillman Drake
GAME THEORY Ken Binmore
GANDHI Bhikhu Parekh
GARDEN HISTORY Gordon Campbell
GENDER HISTORY Antoinette Burton
GENES Jonathan Slack
GENIUS Andrew Robinson
GENOMICS John Archibald
GEOGRAPHY John Matthews and David Herbert
GEOLOGY Jan Zalasiewicz
GEOMETRY Maciej Dunajski
GEOPHYSICAL AND CLIMATE HAZARDS Bill McGuire
GEOPHYSICS William Lowrie
GEOPOLITICS Klaus Dodds
GERMAN LITERATURE Nicholas Boyle
GERMAN PHILOSOPHY Andrew Bowie
THE GHETTO Bryan Cheyette
GLACIATION David J. A. Evans
GLOBAL ECONOMIC HISTORY Robert C. Allen
GLOBAL ISLAM Nile Green
GLOBALIZATION Manfred B. Steger
GOD John Bowker
GÖDEL'S THEOREM A. W. Moore
GOETHE Ritchie Robertson
THE GOTHIC Nick Groom
GOVERNANCE Mark Bevir
GRAVITY Timothy Clifton
THE GREAT DEPRESSION AND THE NEW DEAL Eric Rauchway
THE GULAG Alan Barenberg
HABEAS CORPUS Amanda L. Tyler
HABERMAS James Gordon Finlayson
THE HABSBURG EMPIRE Martyn Rady
HAPPINESS Daniel M. Haybron
THE HARLEM RENAISSANCE Cheryl A. Wall
THE HEBREW BIBLE AS LITERATURE Tod Linafelt
HEGEL Peter Singer
HEIDEGGER Michael Inwood
THE HELLENISTIC AGE Peter Thonemann
HEREDITY John Waller
HERMENEUTICS Jens Zimmermann
HERODOTUS Jennifer T. Roberts
HIEROGLYPHS Penelope Wilson
HINDUISM Kim Knott
HISTORY John H. Arnold
THE HISTORY OF ASTRONOMY Michael Hoskin
THE HISTORY OF CHEMISTRY William H. Brock
THE HISTORY OF CHILDHOOD James Marten
THE HISTORY OF CINEMA Geoffrey Nowell-Smith
THE HISTORY OF COMPUTING Doron Swade
THE HISTORY OF EMOTIONS Thomas Dixon

THE HISTORY OF LIFE
Michael Benton
THE HISTORY OF MATHEMATICS
Jacqueline Stedall
THE HISTORY OF MEDICINE
William Bynum
THE HISTORY OF PHYSICS
J. L. Heilbron
THE HISTORY OF POLITICAL THOUGHT Richard Whatmore
THE HISTORY OF TIME
Leofranc Holford-Strevens
HIV AND AIDS Alan Whiteside
HOBBES Richard Tuck
HOLLYWOOD Peter Decherney
THE HOLY ROMAN EMPIRE
Joachim Whaley
HOME Michael Allen Fox
HOMER Barbara Graziosi
HORACE Llewelyn Morgan
HORMONES Martin Luck
HORROR Darryl Jones
HUMAN ANATOMY
Leslie Klenerman
HUMAN EVOLUTION Bernard Wood
HUMAN PHYSIOLOGY
Jamie A. Davies
HUMAN RESOURCE MANAGEMENT
Adrian Wilkinson
HUMAN RIGHTS Andrew Clapham
HUMANISM Stephen Law
HUME James A. Harris
HUMOUR Noël Carroll
IBN SĪNĀ (AVICENNA)
Peter Adamson
THE ICE AGE Jamie Woodward
IDENTITY Florian Coulmas
IDEOLOGY Michael Freeden
IMAGINATION
Jennifer Gosetti-Ferencei
THE IMMUNE SYSTEM
Paul Klenerman
INDIAN CINEMA
Ashish Rajadhyaksha
INDIAN PHILOSOPHY Sue Hamilton
THE INDUSTRIAL REVOLUTION
Robert C. Allen
INFECTIOUS DISEASE
Marta L. Wayne and Benjamin M. Bolker
INFINITY Ian Stewart
INFORMATION Luciano Floridi
INNOVATION Mark Dodgson and David Gann
INTELLECTUAL PROPERTY
Siva Vaidhyanathan
INTELLIGENCE Ian J. Deary
INTERNATIONAL LAW
Vaughan Lowe
INTERNATIONAL MIGRATION
Khalid Koser
INTERNATIONAL RELATIONS
Christian Reus-Smit
INTERNATIONAL SECURITY
Christopher S. Browning
INSECTS Simon Leather
INVASIVE SPECIES
Julie Lockwood and Dustin Welbourne
IRAN Ali M. Ansari
ISLAM Malise Ruthven
ISLAMIC HISTORY Adam Silverstein
ISLAMIC LAW Mashood A. Baderin
ISOTOPES Rob Ellam
ITALIAN LITERATURE
Peter Hainsworth and David Robey
HENRY JAMES Susan L. Mizruchi
JAPANESE LITERATURE Alan Tansman
JESUS Richard Bauckham
JEWISH HISTORY David N. Myers
JEWISH LITERATURE Ilan Stavans
JOURNALISM Ian Hargreaves
JAMES JOYCE Colin MacCabe
JUDAISM Norman Solomon
JUNG Anthony Stevens
THE JURY Renée Lettow Lerner
KABBALAH Joseph Dan
KAFKA Ritchie Robertson
KANT Roger Scruton
KEYNES Robert Skidelsky
KIERKEGAARD Patrick Gardiner
KNOWLEDGE Jennifer Nagel
THE KORAN Michael Cook
KOREA Michael J. Seth
LAKES Warwick F. Vincent
LANDSCAPE ARCHITECTURE
Ian H. Thompson
LANDSCAPES AND GEOMORPHOLOGY
Andrew Goudie and Heather Viles
LANGUAGES Stephen R. Anderson
LATE ANTIQUITY Gillian Clark

LAW Raymond Wacks
THE LAWS OF THERMODYNAMICS
Peter Atkins
LEADERSHIP Keith Grint
LEARNING Mark Haselgrove
LEIBNIZ Maria Rosa Antognazza
C. S. LEWIS James Como
LIBERALISM Michael Freeden
LIGHT Ian Walmsley
LINCOLN Allen C. Guelzo
LINGUISTICS Peter Matthews
LITERARY THEORY Jonathan Culler
LOCKE John Dunn
LOGIC Graham Priest
LOVE Ronald de Sousa
MARTIN LUTHER Scott H. Hendrix
MACHIAVELLI Quentin Skinner
MADNESS Andrew Scull
MAGIC Owen Davies
MAGNA CARTA Nicholas Vincent
MAGNETISM Stephen Blundell
MALTHUS Donald Winch
MAMMALS T. S. Kemp
MANAGEMENT John Hendry
NELSON MANDELA Elleke Boehmer
MAO Delia Davin
MARINE BIOLOGY Philip V. Mladenov
MARKETING
Kenneth Le Meunier-FitzHugh
THE MARQUIS DE SADE John Phillips
MARTYRDOM Jolyon Mitchell
MARX Peter Singer
MATERIALS Christopher Hall
MATHEMATICAL ANALYSIS
Richard Earl
MATHEMATICAL FINANCE
Mark H. A. Davis
MATHEMATICS
Timothy Gowers
MATTER Geoff Cottrell
THE MAYA Matthew Restall and
Amara Solari
THE MEANING OF LIFE
Terry Eagleton
MEASUREMENT David Hand
MEDICAL ETHICS
Michael Dunn and Tony Hope
MEDICAL LAW Charles Foster
MEDIEVAL BRITAIN
John Gillingham and Ralph A. Griffiths
MEDIEVAL LITERATURE
Elaine Treharne
MEDIEVAL PHILOSOPHY
John Marenbon
MEMORY Jonathan K. Foster
METAPHYSICS Stephen Mumford
METHODISM William J. Abraham
THE MEXICAN REVOLUTION
Alan Knight
MICROBIOLOGY Nicholas P. Money
MICROBIOMES Angela E. Douglas
MICROECONOMICS Avinash Dixit
MICROSCOPY Terence Allen
THE MIDDLE AGES Miri Rubin
MILITARY JUSTICE Eugene R. Fidell
MILITARY STRATEGY
Antulio J. Echevarria II
JOHN STUART MILL Gregory Claeys
MINERALS David Vaughan
MIRACLES Yujin Nagasawa
MODERN ARCHITECTURE
Adam Sharr
MODERN ART David Cottington
MODERN BRAZIL Anthony W. Pereira
MODERN CHINA Rana Mitter
MODERN DRAMA
Kirsten E. Shepherd-Barr
MODERN FRANCE
Vanessa R. Schwartz
MODERN INDIA Craig Jeffrey
MODERN IRELAND Senia Pašeta
MODERN ITALY Anna Cento Bull
MODERN JAPAN
Christopher Goto-Jones
MODERN LATIN AMERICAN
LITERATURE
Roberto González Echevarría
MODERN WAR Richard English
MODERNISM Christopher Butler
MOLECULAR BIOLOGY
Aysha Divan and Janice A. Royds
MOLECULES Philip Ball
MONASTICISM Stephen J. Davis
THE MONGOLS Morris Rossabi
MONTAIGNE William M. Hamlin
MOONS David A. Rothery
MORMONISM
Richard Lyman Bushman
MOUNTAINS Martin F. Price
MUHAMMAD Jonathan A. C. Brown

MULTICULTURALISM Ali Rattansi
MULTILINGUALISM John C. Maher
MUSIC Nicholas Cook
MUSIC AND TECHNOLOGY
Mark Katz
MYTH Robert A. Segal
NANOTECHNOLOGY Philip Moriarty
NAPOLEON David A. Bell
THE NAPOLEONIC WARS
Mike Rapport
NATIONALISM Steven Grosby
NATIVE AMERICAN LITERATURE
Sean Teuton
NAVIGATION Jim Bennett
NAZI GERMANY Jane Caplan
NEGOTIATION Carrie Menkel-Meadow
NEOLIBERALISM Manfred B. Steger and
Ravi K. Roy
NETWORKS Guido Caldarelli and
Michele Catanzaro
THE NEW TESTAMENT
Luke Timothy Johnson
THE NEW TESTAMENT AS
LITERATURE Kyle Keefer
NEWTON Robert Iliffe
NIETZSCHE Michael Tanner
NINETEENTH-CENTURY BRITAIN
Christopher Harvie and
H. C. G. Matthew
THE NORMAN CONQUEST
George Garnett
NORTH AMERICAN INDIANS
Theda Perdue and Michael D. Green
NORTHERN IRELAND
Marc Mulholland
NOTHING Frank Close
NUCLEAR PHYSICS Frank Close
NUCLEAR POWER Maxwell Irvine
NUCLEAR WEAPONS
Joseph M. Siracusa
NUMBER THEORY Robin Wilson
NUMBERS Peter M. Higgins
NUTRITION David A. Bender
OBJECTIVITY Stephen Gaukroger
OBSERVATIONAL ASTRONOMY
Geoff Cottrell
OCEANS Dorrik Stow
THE OLD TESTAMENT
Michael D. Coogan
THE ORCHESTRA D. Kern Holoman
ORGANIC CHEMISTRY
Graham Patrick
ORGANIZATIONS Mary Jo Hatch
ORGANIZED CRIME
Georgios A. Antonopoulos and
Georgios Papanicolaou
ORTHODOX CHRISTIANITY
A. Edward Siecienski
OVID Llewelyn Morgan
PAGANISM Owen Davies
PAKISTAN Pippa Virdee
THE PALESTINIAN-ISRAELI CONFLICT
Martin Bunton
PANDEMICS Christian W. McMillen
PARTICLE PHYSICS Frank Close
PAUL E. P. Sanders
IVAN PAVLOV Daniel P. Todes
PEACE Oliver P. Richmond
PENTECOSTALISM William K. Kay
PERCEPTION Brian Rogers
THE PERIODIC TABLE Eric R. Scerri
PHILOSOPHICAL METHOD
Timothy Williamson
PHILOSOPHY Edward Craig
PHILOSOPHY IN THE ISLAMIC
WORLD Peter Adamson
PHILOSOPHY OF BIOLOGY
Samir Okasha
PHILOSOPHY OF LAW
Raymond Wacks
PHILOSOPHY OF MIND
Barbara Gail Montero
PHILOSOPHY OF PHYSICS
David Wallace
PHILOSOPHY OF SCIENCE
Samir Okasha
PHILOSOPHY OF RELIGION
Tim Bayne
PHOTOGRAPHY Steve Edwards
PHYSICAL CHEMISTRY Peter Atkins
PHYSICS Sidney Perkowitz
PILGRIMAGE Ian Reader
PLAGUE Paul Slack
PLANETARY SYSTEMS
Raymond T. Pierrehumbert
PLANETS David A. Rothery
PLANTS Timothy Walker
PLATE TECTONICS Peter Molnar
SYLVIA PLATH Heather Clark
PLATO Julia Annas

POETRY Bernard O'Donoghue
POLITICAL PHILOSOPHY David Miller
POLITICS Kenneth Minogue
POLYGAMY Sarah M. S. Pearsall
POPULISM Cas Mudde and Cristóbal Rovira Kaltwasser
POSTCOLONIALISM Robert J. C. Young
POSTMODERNISM Christopher Butler
POSTSTRUCTURALISM Catherine Belsey
POVERTY Philip N. Jefferson
PREHISTORY Chris Gosden
PRESOCRATIC PHILOSOPHY Catherine Osborne
PRIVACY Raymond Wacks
PROBABILITY John Haigh
PROGRESSIVISM Walter Nugent
PROHIBITION W. J. Rorabaugh
PROJECTS Andrew Davies
PROTESTANTISM Mark A. Noll
MARCEL PROUST Joshua Landy
PSEUDOSCIENCE Michael D. Gordin
PSYCHIATRY Tom Burns
PSYCHOANALYSIS Daniel Pick
PSYCHOLOGY Gillian Butler and Freda McManus
PSYCHOLOGY OF MUSIC Elizabeth Hellmuth Margulis
PSYCHOPATHY Essi Viding
PSYCHOTHERAPY Tom Burns and Eva Burns-Lundgren
PUBLIC ADMINISTRATION Stella Z. Theodoulou and Ravi K. Roy
PUBLIC HEALTH Virginia Berridge
PURITANISM Francis J. Bremer
THE QUAKERS Pink Dandelion
QUANTUM THEORY John Polkinghorne
RACISM Ali Rattansi
RADIOACTIVITY Claudio Tuniz
RASTAFARI Ennis B. Edmonds
READING Belinda Jack
THE REAGAN REVOLUTION Gil Troy
REALITY Jan Westerhoff
RECONSTRUCTION Allen C. Guelzo
THE REFORMATION Peter Marshall
REFUGEES Gil Loescher
RELATIVITY Russell Stannard
RELIGION Thomas A. Tweed
RELIGION IN AMERICA Timothy Beal
THE RENAISSANCE Jerry Brotton
RENAISSANCE ART Geraldine A. Johnson
RENEWABLE ENERGY Nick Jelley
REPTILES T. S. Kemp
REVOLUTIONS Jack A. Goldstone
RHETORIC Richard Toye
RISK Baruch Fischhoff and John Kadvany
RITUAL Barry Stephenson
RIVERS Nick Middleton
ROBOTICS Alan Winfield
ROCKS Jan Zalasiewicz
ROMAN BRITAIN Peter Salway
THE ROMAN EMPIRE Christopher Kelly
THE ROMAN REPUBLIC David M. Gwynn
ROMANTICISM Michael Ferber
ROUSSEAU Robert Wokler
THE RULE OF LAW Aziz Z. Huq
RUSSELL A. C. Grayling
THE RUSSIAN ECONOMY Richard Connolly
RUSSIAN HISTORY Geoffrey Hosking
RUSSIAN LITERATURE Catriona Kelly
RUSSIAN POLITICS Brian D. Taylor
THE RUSSIAN REVOLUTION S. A. Smith
SAINTS Simon Yarrow
SAMURAI Michael Wert
SAVANNAS Peter A. Furley
SCEPTICISM Duncan Pritchard
SCHIZOPHRENIA Chris Frith and Eve Johnstone
SCHOPENHAUER Christopher Janaway
SCIENCE AND RELIGION Thomas Dixon and Adam R. Shapiro
SCIENCE FICTION David Seed
THE SCIENTIFIC REVOLUTION Lawrence M. Principe
SCOTLAND Rab Houston
SECULARISM Andrew Copson
THE SELF Marya Schechtman
SEXUAL SELECTION Marlene Zuk and Leigh W. Simmons
SEXUALITY Véronique Mottier

WILLIAM SHAKESPEARE
Stanley Wells
SHAKESPEARE'S COMEDIES
Bart van Es
SHAKESPEARE'S SONNETS AND POEMS Jonathan F. S. Post
SHAKESPEARE'S TRAGEDIES
Stanley Wells
GEORGE BERNARD SHAW
Christopher Wixson
MARY SHELLEY Charlotte Gordon
THE SHORT STORY Andrew Kahn
SIKHISM Eleanor Nesbitt
SILENT FILM Donna Kornhaber
THE SILK ROAD James A. Millward
SLANG Jonathon Green
SLEEP Steven W. Lockley and Russell G. Foster
SMELL Matthew Cobb
ADAM SMITH Christopher J. Berry
SOCIAL AND CULTURAL ANTHROPOLOGY
John Monaghan and Peter Just
SOCIAL PSYCHOLOGY Richard J. Crisp
SOCIAL WORK Sally Holland and Jonathan Scourfield
SOCIALISM Michael Newman
SOCIOLINGUISTICS John Edwards
SOCIOLOGY Steve Bruce
SOCRATES C. C. W. Taylor
SOFT MATTER Tom McLeish
SOUND Mike Goldsmith
SOUTHEAST ASIA James R. Rush
THE SOVIET UNION Stephen Lovell
THE SPANISH CIVIL WAR
Helen Graham
SPANISH LITERATURE Jo Labanyi
THE SPARTANS Andrew J. Bayliss
SPINOZA Roger Scruton
SPIRITUALITY Philip Sheldrake
SPORT Mike Cronin
STARS Andrew King
STATISTICS David J. Hand
STEM CELLS Jonathan Slack
STOICISM Brad Inwood
STRUCTURAL ENGINEERING
David Blockley
STUART BRITAIN John Morrill
SUBURBS Carl Abbott
THE SUN Philip Judge
SUPERCONDUCTIVITY
Stephen Blundell
SUPERSTITION Stuart Vyse
SURVEILLANCE David Lyon
SYMMETRY Ian Stewart
SYNAESTHESIA Julia Simner
SYNTHETIC BIOLOGY Jamie A. Davies
SYSTEMS BIOLOGY Eberhard O. Voit
TAXATION Stephen Smith
TEETH Peter S. Ungar
TERRORISM Charles Townshend
THEATRE Marvin Carlson
THEOLOGY David F. Ford
THINKING AND REASONING
Jonathan St B. T. Evans
THOUGHT Tim Bayne
THUCYDIDES Jennifer T. Roberts
TIBETAN BUDDHISM
Matthew T. Kapstein
TIDES David George Bowers and Emyr Martyn Roberts
TIME Jenann Ismael
TOCQUEVILLE Harvey C. Mansfield
J. R. R. TOLKIEN Matthew Townend
LEO TOLSTOY Liza Knapp
TOPOLOGY Richard Earl
TRAGEDY Adrian Poole
TRANSLATION Matthew Reynolds
THE TREATY OF VERSAILLES
Michael S. Neiberg
TRIGONOMETRY Glen Van Brummelen
THE TROJAN WAR Eric H. Cline
ANTHONY TROLLOPE Dinah Birch
TRUST Katherine Hawley
THE TUDORS John Guy
TWENTIETH-CENTURY BRITAIN
Kenneth O. Morgan
TYPOGRAPHY Paul Luna
THE UNITED NATIONS
Jussi M. Hanhimäki
UNIVERSITIES AND COLLEGES
David Palfreyman and Paul Temple
THE U.S. CIVIL WAR Louis P. Masur
THE U.S. CONGRESS Donald A. Ritchie
THE U.S. CONSTITUTION
David J. Bodenhamer
THE U.S. SUPREME COURT
Linda Greenhouse
UTILITARIANISM Katarzyna de Lazari-Radek and Peter Singer

UTOPIANISM Lyman Tower Sargent
VATICAN II Shaun Blanchard and Stephen Bullivant
VETERINARY SCIENCE James Yeates
THE VICTORIANS Martin Hewitt
THE VIKINGS Julian D. Richards
VIOLENCE Philip Dwyer
THE VIRGIN MARY Mary Joan Winn Leith
THE VIRTUES Craig A. Boyd and Kevin Timpe
VIRUSES Dorothy H. Crawford
VOLCANOES Michael J. Branney and Jan Zalasiewicz
VOLTAIRE Nicholas Cronk
WAR AND RELIGION Jolyon Mitchell and Joshua Rey
WAR AND TECHNOLOGY Alex Roland
WATER John Finney
WAVES Mike Goldsmith
WEATHER Storm Dunlop
SIMONE WEIL A. Rebecca Rozelle-Stone
THE WELFARE STATE David Garland
WITCHCRAFT Malcolm Gaskill
WITTGENSTEIN A. C. Grayling
WORK Stephen Fineman
WORLD MUSIC Philip Bohlman
WORLD MYTHOLOGY David Leeming
THE WORLD TRADE ORGANIZATION Amrita Narlikar
WORLD WAR II Gerhard L. Weinberg
WRITING AND SCRIPT Andrew Robinson
ZIONISM Michael Stanislawski
ÉMILE ZOLA Brian Nelson

Available soon:

MEANING Emma Borg and Sarah A. Fisher

For more information visit our website
www.oup.com/vsi/

Aziz Z. Huq

THE RULE OF LAW

A Very Short Introduction

OXFORD
UNIVERSITY PRESS

Oxford University Press is a department of the University of Oxford.
It furthers the University's objective of excellence in research, scholarship,
and education by publishing worldwide. Oxford is a registered trade mark of
Oxford University Press in the UK and in certain other countries.

Published in the United States of America by Oxford University Press
198 Madison Avenue, New York, NY 10016, United States of America.

Library of Congress Cataloging-in-Publication Data
Names: Huq, Aziz Z., author.
Title: The rule of law : a very short introduction / Aziz Z. Huq.
Description: New York : Oxford University Press, 2024. |
Series: Very short introductions | Includes bibliographical references and index.
Identifiers: LCCN 2024013024 (print) | LCCN 2024013025 (ebook) |
ISBN 9780197657423 (paperback) | ISBN 9780197657447 (epub)
Subjects: LCSH: Rule of law.
Classification: LCC K3171 .H87 2024 (print) |
LCC K3171 (ebook) | DDC 340/.11—dc23/eng/20240325
LC record available at https://lccn.loc.gov/2024013024
LC ebook record available at https://lccn.loc.gov/2024013025

Integrated Books International, United States of America

Contents

Preface

This is a very short introduction to an important yet nebulous idea. Politicians, judges, and citizens commonly use the phrase "rule of law" to describe something good flowing from a legal system. What precisely that good is often goes unsaid. Talk of the "rule of law," rather, tends to reflect starkly different hopes for a legal system. In many instances, if not inevitably, that aspiration centers on law acting as a constraint on power, especially the nation-state's fearsome authorities. Rule-of-law talk hence emerges in moments at which a legal system seems under strain. The United Kingdom, for example, experienced such strain during debates over Brexit. The United States, in contrast, had one rule of law "crisis" after the terror attacks on September 11, 2001, and a second due to the efforts of former president Donald Trump to remain in office after losing a democratic election. Yet there is widespread disagreement on what state abuse the rule of law forestalls. This disagreement starts within an Anglo-American legal tradition. It then spills out globally. Given its breadth and diversity, it is tempting to dismiss the ensuing debate as the empty chatter of governing elites from the DC Beltway to Beijing.

The question posed by this book is what would be lost if all talk of the rule of the law was rejected as hollow. Consider the events of September 2022, when Iranian women took to the streets protesting their arbitrary and despotic handling by the so-called morality police. Their complaint, at the core, reverberated in terms the rule-of-law tradition provides. Without that tradition, however, would their plight have been less legible and urgent? Does talk of "human rights" or "democracy" offer a complete substitute for the "rule of law"? Or does the latter capture something distinctive about the misuse of state power that other terms miss? Beyond Iran, the early twentieth century has been a period of sharp, destabilizing spasms as a result of terrorism, macroeconomic crisis, pandemics, autocratic populism, and climate change. Even in the historic homelands, the rule of law (however understood) is seen as being under pressure. For better or worse, this means that deciding on whether the rule of law matters, and if so how, is no longer the preserve of lawyers, scholars, and judges. It is a problem for us all.

The modest aspiration of this little book is to help readers understand whether, how, and why the rule of law might still matter to them in this turbulent moment. While I refrain from endorsing a particular understanding of the rule of law, I hope what follows is a fair-minded mapping of the historical heft and present difficulty of that term.

Acknowledgments

I am grateful to David Dyzenhaus, Tom Ginsburg, Martin Loughlin, Gerald Postema, and two anonymous reviewers for Oxford University Press, for reading the manuscript and giving insightful comments. Parts of the manuscript benefited from workshops at the University of Chicago and NYU Law School. Nancy Toff guided the book wisely and gave terrific feedback. Margaret, Kian, and Corin—as ever—made this book possible and worthwhile.

Chapter 1
Why does the rule of law matter?

The phrase "rule of law" started to be used widely at the end of the nineteenth century within the work of English jurist Albert Venn Dicey. In the tradition that Dicey seeded, "rule of law" is used to describe a legal system in good working order. It is an explicitly evaluative term. It thus carries a moral charge. To be more precise, it reflects a judgment on how a legal system ideally would work, and what it ideally should do. As such, the English language tradition of thinking about the rule of law overlaps with, while also taking distinct turns from, several other intellectual traditions. These include similar traditions in German thinking about the *Rechtsstaat* and French reflection on *L'État de droit*. This short book isolates and examines the genealogy of English-language debate centered around the phrase "rule of law." It addresses the distinctive ethical contribution offered by this phrase, largely setting aside how the same questions are framed and resolved in other traditions.

Is there a common thread to the rule-of-law tradition beyond its ethical character? A core rule-of-law aspiration is that law can and should constrain how power is flexed, especially by the state. Yet how or when this happens is disputed and murky. Disagreement persists, for example, as to whether the rule of law is a matter of "how" law is used, or "why" it is deployed. People with profoundly different moral commitments and beliefs can and do hoist the rule of law as a banner—or swing it as a cudgel. Such disagreements, however, do not undermine the rule of law's relevance. To the contrary, they show that the rule of law can still be deployed as a way of framing and evaluating the substantive moral ends of law and legal systems. It is, in that sense, akin to the word "justice," which offers an indispensable, and so necessarily vague, platform for making moral claims of society at large.

One reason for disagreement is that "the law" itself is a very complex social practice. A modern legal system is inevitably a blend of statutes, a "common law" created by judges in lines of cases, regulations issued by the executive, and widely shared precepts and social practices. The rule of law might pick out only some of these modalities as particularly important. Law is also usually viewed as distinct and autonomous from other bodies of rules, such as social mores or religious dictates. At the same time, it is supposed to be comprehensive in reach and supreme over the other bodies of rules within a given nation. A modern legal system also has many moving parts: there are formal legal institutions, such as legislatures, courts, and officials; there are received wisdoms and age-old customs; and there is often tacit knowledge about the way things should be done. All these can be assembled in different ways. But a common assumption in talk of the rule of law is the existence of a single standard, applicable across all this variation. Is that demanding assumption, which often goes unnoticed and undefended, viable though? Or do different legal systems, which are made up of different sorts of institutions, embody different versions of the rule of law?

Uncertainty about what the rule of law means only grows upon an examination of how the phrase is used in practice. It is not only on the lips of those protesting unjust and arbitrary violence around the world. It also figures centrally in many authoritative statements about legal systems today. A survey of such usage quickly uncovers startling and unlikely bedfellows. The rule of law, it would seem, has only friends, but no enemies.

The phrase "rule of law" figures prominently in British law. When the United Kingdom enacted the Constitutional Reform Act in 2005, the UK Parliament opened it by affirming "the existing constitutional principle of the rule of law" and "the Lord Chancellor's existing constitutional role in relation to that principle." The Lord Chancellor is appointed by the monarch to head the Ministry of Justice and the English judiciary. He or she takes an oath to respect the rule of law and the independence of the judiciary. But no definition of the rule of law is to be found in a parliamentary enactment.

Talk of "the rule of law" as a distinct ideal, which no other phrase can convey, has spread well beyond the English-speaking world. Consider two events from 1997. That year, then World Bank president James Wolfensohn gave an oft-quoted speech on the rule of law. He called for every government seeking the bank's aid to have "a comprehensive legal system that is effectively, impartially and cleanly administered by a well-functioning, honest and impartial judicial and legal system." Both the World Bank and the International Monetary Fund thereafter placed greater weight upon, and fatter wads of cash behind, the "rule of law" plank of their programming. This new concern embodied an influential understanding of how to count as a respectable nation-state in the post–Cold War order then coming into view. In addition, in 1997 president and party general secretary Jiang Zemin persuaded the Fifteenth Party Congress of the Chinese Communist Party to embrace the rule of law as "the basic strategy employed by the Party in leading the people." Two years later, Jiang secured a change to Article 5 of China's 1982 Constitution, which was amended to say that the country was governed "according to law" as "a socialist country under rule of law." Over the following decade, post-Soviet nations also engaged in constitutional change invoking the rule of law. Hungary, for example, signaled its exit from Communist rule with a new constitution promising a new "independent, democratic State under the rule of law."

Few modern captains of state fail to doff their hats to the rule of law. Yet can a single phrase retain a cohesive meaning after enduring embraces so numerous and so promiscuous? Once a term or phrase has been unconditionally claimed by the UK Parliament, the Chinese Communist Party, and the World Bank, is there anything of common substance left to it? Or has the rule of law been reduced by its success to hollow and meaningless cant?

The stakes of the rule of law

The rule of law can be scrutinized from the other side of the telescope—from the vantage point of those who bear it or benefit from it. Despite its slipperiness, the notion of the rule of law as some kind of demand upon law and the legal system has real-world stakes. For many ordinary people, there is a sense that the term "rule of law" picks out something that is a necessary foundation for a stable, orderly life. That is, if you ask *them* whether the rule of law matters, they will recognize that it does, even if it is hard for them to define. It characterizes a situation in which they can plan and execute the long-term projects involved in family, work, and friendship. In this sense, the rule of law seems in profound contemporary peril along several fronts. The early twenty-first century has been characterized by a cascade of shocks, including terrorism, wars, pandemics, climate change, democratic erosion, and global macroeconomic crisis. Sharp ideological conflict over the basic terms of political life persists. Just one such shock can undermine a legal system, robbing people of the benefits of the rule of law. So the contemporary moment can plausibly be understood as a plurality of overlapping rule-of-law crises. At the very moment legality rhetoric seems most vacuous, it also seems most needed.

For better or worse, the default modern vehicle for producing legality is the nation-state. For many, the rule of law fails simply because their state fails. State-building efforts by wealthy Western coalitions in both Afghanistan and Iraq, for example, notoriously faltered in the early twenty-first century. Despite enacting a provisional constitution in 2011, and forging a federal government in 2012, the Somalian state has struggled against al-Shabaab and the separatist Somaliland movement. These examples are prominent, but not unique. In 2008, a UN study calculated, no less than 51 percent of the globe's populace lived in "failed, weak, or fragile" states. Religious or tribal rule at times fills the gap. But few perceive statelessness as anything less than a wholesale rule-of-law failure. The question of "state-building"—i.e., creating functioning legal offices from the ground up—is hence related in an important way to the rule of law. But the failures of Afghanistan and Iraq, despite massive influxes of international assistance, point to the fact that the practice and theory of intentional state-building is at best uncertain. The lingering haze from ordinance above Kabul and Baghdad suggests that we still know too little to offer confident prescriptions.

A violent anarchy can also provoke the state into its own, extralegal violence. This strains the rule of law in a second way. Consider recent experience in the Philippines. In 2016 then new president Rodrigo Duterte declared that he would respond without mercy to a tide of drug-related, violent crime. Brushing aside concerns about legality, he contended that "sometimes the rule of law becomes a stupid proposition." His approach to policing was simple: demand surrender, and if no compliance followed, "[s]hoot them dead." By March 2019, the Philippine police reported that they had killed some 29,000 suspects, many in anti-narcotics operations, during the Duterte presidency. Duterte's "shoot to kill" policy, and his comments on crime, created a sense that police officers had near unlimited discretion to use violence against a civilian population. Violence could be used on a whim, without regard to its cost for bystanders or its benefits to crime control.

A third sort of crisis in the rule of law unfolds within the seemingly peaceful polity. It can happen when a tide of democratic enthusiasm hits the ordinary guardrails of politics. This sort of conflict becomes more likely when leaders claim a "populist" mandate to speak for the people against so-called elites. Such a conflict arose during the tortuous series of political and legal battles following the UK's 2016 referendum on leaving the European Union. In August 2019 Prime Minister Boris Johnson advised Queen Elizabeth II to suspend Parliament for roughly five weeks. To his political opponents, Johnson's prorogation (as this is known) was a transparent dodge to swerve around parliamentary scrutiny of his Brexit plans. To his defenders, it was a judicious exercise of prime ministerial prerogative to cut a Gordian knot blocking British politics. A judicial challenge to the suspension duly came. In September 2019 the UK Supreme Court ruled unanimously that Johnson's suspension was "outside the powers of the Prime Minister," and so null and of no effect. Opinion was starkly divided: Brexit's advocates, including the emeritus Oxford don John Finnis, contended that the court's decision to order Parliament back in session was an unprecedented intrusion of the judiciary into democratic politics. An early proponent of proroguing Parliament in the popular press, Finnis contended that the court's ruling was "a threat to the rule of law." To those more sympathetic to the prospect of continuing EU membership, the court's ruling was "entirely a victory for the rule of law." Anything less, they suggested, would have been a "dereliction" of the court's duty. What's important here is not who is correct. Rather, the point to stress is the way that debate about the UK Supreme Court's ruling was in effect a debate about what the rule of law demanded.

A fourth sort of challenge to the rule of law has a different gravity. It arises when a government pauses the ordinary operation of its legal system to address a perceived emergency or crisis. The laws that empower official action remain in effect. Rules that restrain the state, however, fall away as officials use their practical power in wide-reaching, novel, and potentially illegal ways. What ensues can encompass just a few people. Or it can blanket an entire population. Well-known examples of the first come from the so-called war on terror. Terrorism suspects after the September 11, 2001, attacks were detained outside the ordinary processes of the law in places such as HM Prison Belmarsh in the United Kingdom and the US naval base at Guantánamo Bay, Cuba. When Lord Johan Steyn derisively called that Cuban prison a "legal black hole," he captured the gist of the rule-of-law complaint about such severe and targeted derogation.

The second scenario is illustrated, according to libertarian critics, by coercive elements of the governmental responses to the COVID-19 pandemic. Lockdowns and mask mandates were criticized as species of tyranny. In one country in particular, the pandemic emergency also became a pathway for unraveling democratic institutions. In May 2020 the Hungarian parliament voted to allow its premier, Viktor Orbán, to rule by decree for an indefinite period. When the legislature ended the state of emergency two months later, it did not withdraw the premier's newly-minted "extraordinary and unlimited government powers" to rule by decree. One commentator characterized the presidential decree powers that permanently ensued as "a violation of the most basic idea of the rule of law: that no man should be above the law."

In each of these four situations, it could plausibly be argued—and indeed was argued—that the rule of law was in mortal peril. It is not at all clear that those affected could even have articulated their moral critique without invoking the rule of law, or something very like it. But at the same time, it is quite plain that these situations all involved very different stakes. The law played quite a different role in Manila, Budapest, and London. Not all these situations were characterized by an absolute absence of law. Despite Lord Steyn's strong condemnation, even prison facilities such as Guantánamo Bay rest on a web of treaties, contracts, statutes, and regulations. The alleged threat to law also arose from different corners. In Somalia, it was private violence. In Manila, it was the state's guns and jackboots. In London, it was (depending on your perspective) a bejeweled jurist or a mop-topped populist prime minister. And in Budapest, it was a legislature conniving with a self-proclaimed illiberal leader. How then can a single phrase, "the rule of law," encapsulate all these situations? Is it a virtue, or a vice, that the rule of law, seemingly without strain, can be bent to fit all these different scenarios?

The breadth of the rule of law makes it an essential tool of praise or criticism. But its very capaciousness makes it an exceptionally hard idea to pin down. A central challenge in thinking about the rule of law involves pulling out a common thread that can link together the diversity of cases.

Defining the rule of law

How then do we make sense of the rule of law? To begin with, it is necessary to recognize a difficult threshold issue. Common usages of "rule of law" obviously rely on some idea of what counts as "law" in the first place. But the project of defining what counts as law is in fact quite a challenging one. Social ordering through general rules takes many forms across different societies. It is not always clear when the label "law" is apt. Take the case of Amdo, the historically Tibetan region in what is now Qinghai Province of China. Nomadic tribes there settled disputes in formal gatherings, invoking arguments about injury and status while haggling over appropriate compensation without the benefit of an authoritative written text. Is it merely narrow-minded to say there was no law at stake there? Scholars disagree. Certainly, the mere fact that what the nomads of Amdo do is different from what happens at the Old Bailey in London or at the US Supreme Court in Washington, DC, ought not alone disqualify them from the coverage of the term "law." Indeed, drawing a sharp boundary around the category of law often reflects a choked parochialism.

There is a second and related threshold problem: The "law" might be defined in a way that overlaps with demands imposed by the rule of law. But if "law" and the "rule of law" mean the same thing, how can the latter be used as a term of evaluation and as a basis for blame or praise? Surely a complaint about the rule of law would just boil down to the factual claim that there was no law at work. The problem comes into focus if law is defined as a set of guiding commands characterized by clarity, stability, and publicity, and the rule of law is understood in terms of those same qualities. Another possibility is that law could be defined in a way set forth by the twentieth-century British legal scholar H. L. A. Hart. According to Hart's influential theory, a legal system exists only if there is a class of officials who abide by a set of fundamental criteria about what counts as law. If we define the rule of law in terms of rule-following by officials, there is a sense in which its existence tautologically follows from Hart's definition of a modern legal system. So there are a couple of ways in which the concept of law and the definition of the rule of law might be taken to overlap in whole or part.

But starting off with a pair of overlapping understandings of law and the rule of law invites confusion. It might shut down the project of evaluating law, rather than just describing it. It also does not enhance understandings of the many ways in which the rule of law is used in practice as a label assigning praise or blame. Perhaps reflection about the rule of law will lead to a conclusion that no such overlap exists. Or else, perhaps if there is an absence of the rule of law, we should not talk of a flawed legal order. We should instead concede that there is no law at all. (This does not, however, fit cases such as Johnson's prorogation or Orbán's decree power.) But, at least to start with, it is useful to distinguish between the description of law or a legal system, on the one hand, and the evaluative standard labeled the "rule of law," on the other.

The best way of exploring the ideal of the rule of law given these concerns is to start with some core cases of the term "law" in action, and then ask what it would mean to apply the "rule of law" to those facts. A common trait of the law in action in the debates about the Philippines, the United Kingdom, and Hungary is simply this: there is an official action by a modern national state or one of its component parts, whether by legislation, regulation, or sheer physical force. The rule of law is, as the term is applied in this context, a way of evaluating such action. Or else the rule of law could be applied to demand action by the state. It can thus be wanting when the state recedes completely and fails to check violent official behavior. Or else it is implicated when the state uses certain tools but not others. State law takes many forms. Law is at work in Johnson's suspension of Parliament and Orbán's pandemic degrees. It is also at stake when judges exercise their discretionary authority. It was in play, for example, when Brazilian judge Alexandre de Moraes ordered the arrests of eight prominent businessmen based on their heated WhatsApp messages just before the October 2022 presidential election. The differences between these forms need not overly detain us now. But it is worth noting that different accounts of the rule of law might suggest a reason for preferring one form over others.

If the core case in which the rule of law is in play involves the state, does the rule of law have nothing to say about powerful private actors? The failed state dishonors the rule of law by its inaction. What then of the injuries received by a person beaten by their intimate partner? Should the idea of the rule of law extend to cases of private violence where the state could, but does not, intervene? Very plausibly, a description of the rule of law that omits such cases has a misogynistic tilt, because it fails disproportionately to reckon with women's lived experience of violence in particular. Another possibility of concern is that powerful private actors may simply bend statutory law to their preferences. For example, in 2021 the social media company Facebook decided to counter the threat of regulation in Australia by shutting down its news feed in that country. Facebook rescinded its ban only after getting the Australian government's assurance that the platform's content moderation policies would not be "subject to forced negotiation." It is surely plausible to ask whether Facebook's action thwarted the rule of law in Australia without thinking that Facebook is itself a "state." So the fact that state action lies at the core of rule-of-law thinking need not refute the possibility that peripheral cases involve capricious private power.

All that being said, there is still a good reason to start with the actions of a president, a legislator, a police officer, or a bureaucrat. These present the paradigmatic scenarios that have provoked debate about the rule of law. Extending the concept to other domains, where the state is absent, should happen only after we have understood the core applications of that idea.

Chapter 2
Seeding the rule of law

In an essay titled "Kafka and His Precursors," the Argentinian fabulist Jorge Luis Borges assembled a slate of literary works anticipating themes and ideas later found in the novels and tales of the Czech writer Franz Kafka. These precursors, observed Borges, resembled Kafka. But otherwise they were quite dissimilar. The thread tying them together, explained the Argentinian, was called into existence only when Kafka put pen to paper. His work thus "modifies our conception of the past."

Our debates today about the rule of law emerge from ideas seeded in ancient and early modern texts, in the works of the ancient Greek thinker Aristotle, the French aristocrat and proto-sociologist Charles-Louis de Secondat (known too as Montesquieu), and the English Whig thinker, political activist, and imperial administrator John Locke. Others could be added to the list. The Florentine diplomat Niccolò Machiavelli and the medieval English jurist Sir John Fortescue, for example, have also been conscripted into this camp of precursors. These thinkers did not use the phrase "rule of law," but nevertheless are commonly perceived as its forebearers. Further, it has been common to suggest that early English legal texts, such as the Magna Carta, anticipate the rule of law. Anglo-American lawyers are especially fond of dwelling on that document, although not always in ways that reflect knowledge of its content or context.

In approaching all these older works, it is useful to keep Borges's wisdom in mind. There is no single plumb line to drop from contemporary debates back into the past. Ancient and early modern writers had concerns quite different from ours. The societies in which they lived, and the earthly powers that worried them, are often alien to our experience. Most importantly, the landscapes of power, whether political or economic, are quite different now from back in the past. A modern state characterized by firm territorial control, deep bureaucratic reserves, and the ability to intervene and shape intimate facets of people's lives emerged only in the late nineteenth century—well after these works were written. Capitalism, a system in which even the necessities of life are produced for profit-oriented exchange, was only an inkling in the early modern era. It did not shape the lives of any precursor rule of law theorist in the way that its neoliberal form deeply shapes our lives today. The ferociously globalized, finance-heavy, and crisis-prone modern world would have seemed fantastical if conjured in yesteryear.

Our problems are thus not necessarily the problems haunting earlier texts. If we find precursors of *our* rule of law in their work, we must be cautious before assuming earlier writers understood those ideas in the same way that we do. The gap is greatest with Magna Carta. A contract between monarch and barons is an oddly inapt forebearer for the rule of law, especially given the charter's role in stabilizing English feudal relations. Its invocation is less historically acute than it is forelock-tugging deference to an imagined national story. But even when approaching the work of Aristotle, Montesquieu, and Locke, it is necessary to keep in mind the gulf between our world and theirs. We should, in Borges's spirit, attend to suggestive intimations of our ideas. We should not seek an embryonic version of the rule of law ready to be plucked from history's rich and loamy soil.

In particular, we do well to recall that all three writers addressed in this chapter, Aristotle, Montesquieu, and Locke, were engaged in philosophical projects distinct and alien from ours. Both Aristotle and Montesquieu were refining taxonomies of political regime types that they had been able to observe in their worlds. But they did so with different ends in mind. Aristotle may well have been preparing a specialized text for use in teaching at the Lyceum, a school in Athens. The polymath French aristocrat Montesquieu spoke to an international audience of scholarly peers interested both in politics and in what we would today call the natural world. He was alert to the environment's shaping influence on human affairs, as well as to the ways in which political institutions could work differently under varying ecological conditions. In contrast to those reflective enterprises, Locke's ambition was polemic. He was engaged in a high-stakes battle with a vision of divinely credentialed monarchy offered by King Charles I of England and Scotland, forcefully recapitulated in Sir Robert Filmer's tract *Patriarchia*, on the behalf of a new, property-owning capitalist vision of society. Not one of these thinkers was trying to tease out law's ideal role in anything like a modern society. We plunder the past at our peril. Perhaps it serves our present ends, but the hazards of misapprehension can never quite be dispelled.

Aristotle

Biography is not theory. But there is a little story about the Greek scholar Aristotle that might cast some light on his personal view of the law as a comprehensive regulatory system. In 323 BCE the emperor Alexander died and the Greek city-states, including Athens, rose in general revolt against the Macedonian yoke. In this febrile moment, a charge of impiety was lodged against the teacher and scholar Aristotle, originally of Stagira but for decades a resident of Athens. Aristotle chose to flee Athens for the city of Chalcis on the nearby island of Euboea. With Socrates's death in mind, he remarked that his flight had saved Athens from sinning a second time against philosophy—the first time, of course, being the trial and execution of Socrates. So much, then, for the binding moral force of law!

If Aristotle is the origin of our ideal of the rule of law, this little tale might lead us to anticipate something less than a full-throated endorsement of legality above all else. And so indeed it is. Fragments of Aristotle's work can be, and are, picked out, shucked of context, and then paraded as evidence that he was the rule of law's first paladin. More carefully read, however, his work is more ambiguous. Its force comes from the questions it stages, and the fraught choice between "rule by law" and "rule by men" (for it would be anachronistic and inaccurate to say "rule by people") that it frames, rather than a single answer to that choice.

Aristotle's surviving corpus of writing is only a portion of his original scholarly work. His most important comments on the role that law should play are to be found in his *Politics*. Two other texts, the *Nicomachean Ethics* and *Rhetoric*, contain some suggestive comments about the relation of law to justice. They contend, for example, that laws are more desirable than ad hoc decision-making, because they tend to be made after "long consideration" and reflection. But it is *Politics* that offers the most sustained, valuable reflection on what would come to be called the rule of law.

In ancient catalogs of classical texts, *Politics* is described as a "course of lectures." It may also have been written for an audience beyond the Lyceum's students. One of its core contributions is a taxonomy of what today might be called "constitutional" regimes, or, in the Greek, *politeia*. In this classification, Aristotle is concerned not just to clarify differences between various kinds of regimes that he observed. He also is interested in which *politeia* was to be preferred. Law enters in insofar as it relates to the deeper choice between regimes. The contrast between the rule of law and the rule of man is thus not staged for its own sake. Instead, Aristotle introduces it for the light it casts on the background choice among different *politeia*.

Aristotle's taxonomy of *politeia* turns on who, and how many, govern. There are three main regime types. In a monarchy, the one rules. In an aristocracy, it is the few. And in a "polity," it is the multitude. These are ideal types. Each describes a well-functioning *politeia*. Each also has a degenerate form. Respectively, these are tyranny, oligarchy, and democracy. Law enters the picture as Aristotle reflects upon the contrasts, and continuities, between these regime types. It is regarding the first form—monarchy—that he raises the quandary of "whether it is more advantageous to be ruled by the best man or by the best law." The question is not easy for him to answer, even as applied to monarchy. Instead, his analysis shuttles back and forth evincing restless dissatisfaction about each potential resting point.

To begin with, he observes that it is foolish to be governed always with rigid written rules (the Greek is *kala grammata*). The use of a formula fixed in advance in writing means giving up on adaptability and flexibility. It means ignoring changing conditions and new learning. Yet he also concedes that rigid rules might sometimes be valuable. They rule out "the passionate elements" that distort our on-the-spot judgment. Reflecting upon this risk of contorting passions, Aristotle spins a further distinction. A single ruler might easily be swayed by passion. But a collectivity often "judges many matters better than any single person." (Many minds are better than one—a thought that would be formalized many centuries later by the French thinker Condorcet.) The choice between the rule of general law and the particularistic judgment of a ruler turns on the numerosity, and also the quality, of individual minds making the judgment. Lest this is thought to settle the matter, Aristotle then draws in a final difficulty: perhaps there are things that law simply cannot do. To legislate "concerning matters of deliberation is impossible." What Aristotle does not say is how to discern when law is useful and when its application is "impossible." What counts as a matter best left to deliberation is thus left murky.

All this is hardly a clear definition or a ringing endorsement of the rule of law. Aristotle also declines to give us much detail on where the proper domain of law ends. Its utility is a relative, not an absolute, matter. The quality of available alternatives matters. As the American political theorist Judith Shklar noted, one lesson to draw from Aristotle is that what matters is not so much the choice between fixed law and fickle men, but the choice between men. A "constant disposition to act fairly and lawfully" elicits justice, whether or not there are *kala grammata*, "written rules." Virtue, not institutional design, is key.

Another enduring implication of Aristotle's reasoning is the very notion of a dichotomy between the rule of law and rule by men. This notion was captured by the second American president, John Adams, in his famous distinction between a government of laws and a government of men. Quite what this gap portends, though, is not entirely clear, regardless of the formulation. For Aristotle, the law is both general in scope and written in form (*kala grammata* again). The rule of men has neither of these qualities. Further, each form of rule seems to rest upon and elicit distinctive motives. Law for Aristotle is impartiality. It is "intellect without appetite." And it is assuredly not governed by the appetites and passions of a specific person. With these passages in mind, one influential reading of Aristotle's argument underscores the general desirability of across-the-board rules, rather than particularistic judgments. The late Justice Antonin Scalia of the US Supreme Court, for example, was rather taken by that thought. But as Shklar's reading shows, it is not the only one available, or necessarily the best.

Locke

In the centuries after Aristotle, a disparate range of theorists touched on ideas related to the rule of law. The Roman lawyer and statesman Cicero, for example, praised the value of law as his Republic crumpled and dissolved. Writings attributed to the medieval English official Henry de Bracton invoked the image of law as a "bridle" that governed and directed royal power. And in sixteenth-century Florence, Machiavelli would reflect on the history of Cicero's Roman Republic and its relation to law. One of his intriguing conclusions was that it was the very clash between the plebeians and the wealthy of the city that had led to the creation of Roman "legislation favorable to liberty." But it was not until the writings of Locke in seventeenth-century England that something like the ideal of the rule of law became a central focus of political thinking.

England had a rough seventeenth century. From afar, many thought it was becoming a failed state. Writing in 1652, an anonymous Dutch pamphleteer labeled the island nation "Devilland" because of its anarchic and violent politics. These were varied and bloody. There was brutal civil war, regicide, a novel experiment in republican government through a protectorate, a brutal imperial sally through Ireland, a kingly restoration, and a "glorious" grab of the crown by a Dutch nobleman at the behest of a querulously anti-Catholic Parliament. We are beneficiaries of all this turmoil, which produced striking works of political thought that still shape understandings of law and government. This was the era not just of John Locke, but also Thomas Hobbes.

Hobbes once joked that "fear and I were born twins." His mother had gone into labor, it is said, upon hearing of the shocking approach of the Spanish Armada in April 1588. Whether this little tale is true or not, his *Leviathan* identified law as a ferociously strong binding force emanating from the sovereign and wrapping tight the citizen—even as Hobbes perceived only evanescent bindings limiting the sovereign. For Hobbes, law's coin was the command of the sovereign. It bound only the citizenry, not the leviathan. If that sovereign enacted a statute that violated a law of nature, well, that was a matter between God and the sovereign.

We know surprisingly little of what John Locke thought of Hobbes's work. Locke himself was a physician, political activist, and colonial bureaucrat. He worked in the mid-seventeenth century under the patronage of the prominent Whig politician Anthony Ashley Cooper, the Earl of Shaftesbury. It is known that Locke owned a copy of Hobbes's great work *Leviathan*. But he left remarkably little direct written evidence of his engagement with Hobbes's arguments. In the political theorist John Dunn's words, he "merely and blandly" ignored them in his equally renowned *Second Treatise of Government*. Yet whatever the historical evidence ultimately reveals, Locke's treatment of law provides a striking juxtaposition to Hobbes's sober and pessimistic view. It therefore offers a more promising seed for fleshing out the rule of law.

Like Aristotle, Locke had cause to fear the law. In 1683 a plot was discovered to ambush and kill King Charles II as he passed Rye House in Hertfordshire. Locke was suspected of involvement. With Shaftesbury, he decamped promptly to the Netherlands. *Second Treatise* was published anonymously in 1689, although the conventional view is that it had been written some years earlier. Whatever the exact timing of the book's composition, the shadow of a cruel, potentially tyrannous ruler seems to profoundly shape its arguments.

Like Hobbes, Locke starts with the needfulness of the state. For Locke, formal collective arrangements for government in the form of a state are necessary to vindicate the pre-political rights to property in one's own person and the fruit of one's labors. Unlike Hobbes, Locke thinks that it would make no sense for men to quit their pre-political state if all but the sovereign were thereafter "under the restraint of law." He mocks the idea that people would take pains to avoid the hazards of "pole-cats, or foxes," only to allow themselves to be "devoured by lions." If Hobbes gestured generally to what would come to be known as rule *by* law, Locke took a step toward the modern understanding of the rule *of* law by explaining the justification for law as a restraint on the sovereign.

Government, formed by the consent of the people and operating through majority rule, is not unbounded in authority. Instead, Locke inscribes a distinction between "extemporary, arbitrary degrees" and "promulgated, standing laws, and known, authorized judges." A compulsion for standing laws, and a repudiation of arbitrary power, flows simply from a logic of consensual transition from a pre-political "state of nature" to a collective life under the state's shield. Rationally, one agrees to this move only if personal and property rights are protected effectively. But people disagree about how these rights are defined under the law of nature. If a Hobbesian sovereign had the power to arbitrarily settle those disputes, citizens would be exposed once more to the unjustified loss of the very rights they joined the polity to vindicate. What this means for Locke is not simply that the law must govern, but that the law must also be "promulgated" and "established." There must be "one rule for rich and poor," and it can have no ultimate purpose except "the good of the people." Further, consistent with his accent upon property's primacy, the law cannot take a person's property away without his or her consent. It is not entirely clear from Locke's argument how this last commitment can in practice be realized. Locke, after all, recognizes that property rights can be ambiguous and so controverted in practice. By hedging the sovereign's power with property, he injects a highly contested substantive limit into the definition of the lawful state. But he does not explain how the ensuing disagreements will be resolved without fresh, disabling conflict.

Locke does not use the phrase "rule of law." His aim was not to theorize anything by that name, or of that ilk. He was instead asking what traits a just state must have to induce rational consent from its citizens. As with other such "social contract" arguments, this framing conduces to different answers depending on what assumptions we make about the pre-political world. Locke himself well understood, and explicitly acknowledged, that his story of the origins and scope of pre-political property rights was especially fraught with difficulty.

Yet even if his aim lay elsewhere, Locke made space for a sense of what law might ideally do. As with Aristotle's *Politics*, there is an emphasis on law's generality and the existence of a definite written form. Added to that is a notion of reciprocity absent from Hobbes: for law to serve its foundational ends, it must bind sovereign as well as citizen. Indeed, it must bind the sovereign in specific ways, ruling out "arbitrary" violence and property deprivations. Not all these elements need to run together. To the contrary, a fruitful way of understanding Locke's *Second Treatise* is as posing a vital question: What traits must law have to make it rational for people to bind themselves to a polity in which that law authorizes the use of force against them?

Montesquieu

The Baron de La Brède et de Montesquieu, Charles-Louis de Secondat, sat on the other side of the law from Aristotle and Locke. He was born—as it happened in the year Locke's *Second Treatise* was published—into a propertied noble family in Bordeaux, in southeastern France. Unlike Locke or Aristotle, Montesquieu lived through a period of relative stability and calm. Successful contestation of monarchical authority in France was not yet on the horizon when he wrote. Instead, Montesquieu served for the 11 years beginning in 1711 as *président à mortier*, the title given to the principle judicial office of the local *parlement*. In this capacity, he presided over a criminal division called the *Tournelle*, inflicting punishments such as executions, deportations, and service in the galleys. He oversaw investigations in which torture was a normal step in the judicial process. Yet his novel *Persian Letters*, written during this era, also reflected an abiding horror of despotism, or absolute power, and the fearfulness and iniquities into which it would inevitably lead.

His 1748 masterwork, *The Spirit of the Laws*, is not a singular, sustained argument. It is more a cabinet of wonders built of Montesquieu's wide reading in history, politics, and the natural sciences. It offers a vast and varied taxonomy of social rules and procedures, with an eye to explaining how they evolved in a particular society. A first part of the book offers yet another taxonomy of regime types, distinct from Aristotle's, but still with attention to the role of law in each. A second element considers how nature and culture shape or limit societies. For Montesquieu, law is part of a social whole molded not just by deliberate human decision but also by the natural world. Indeed, his majestically vague definition of "law" as "the necessary relations deriving from the nature of things" illustrates a resistance to sharp divisions between the natural and the engineered social worlds. The last five chapters of the book offer an extended study of Roman and early French laws of succession as an illustration of how law is best studied.

The Spirit of the Laws follows Aristotle's *Politics* in being organized around a taxonomy of regime types. Again, the role that law plays is considered only in relation to specific regimes. There is no pretense that one can unroot "law" from the specific arrangements for governing in which it is embedded, or assign it transcendent, enduring qualities. This has important implications for Montesquieu. It is not just that law must be understood in situ, rather than as a brooding generality stripped of local particulars. It is also that law ought to be tailored to the quirks of the particular society to which it extends. And since the laws must be "appropriate" to the people for whom they are made, Montesquieu is skeptical that the laws of one nation can be uprooted and repotted in the soil of another. This sense of law's geographically specific character has largely been lost from contemporary thinking about the rule of law.

Montesquieu calls the three possible forms of government republican, monarchical, and despotic. The principle distinction between them is not the same as Aristotle's. It does not depend upon *who* wields power. Rather, law enters the picture as part of how regimes are defined and distinguished. This can most clearly be seen in Montesquieu's explanation of how monarchy and despotism differ. Both involve the rule of one person. But in despotism, there is no "fundamental law" guiding and channeling political power. Instead, in despotism there "are no laws." It is the despot's "wills and caprices" all the way down. In a monarchy, in contrast, the prince's powers are exercised through "established laws." Invoking the France of his day, Montesquieu conjured an image of royal power flowing through "intermediate, subordinate, and dependent powers." A monarchy also has a depository of laws. It uses administrative bodies, like the *parlement* in which Montesquieu sat, as tools to ensure that the laws are followed. Lest these distinctions between monarchy and despotism seem trivial, Montesquieu identifies two different defining principles for monarchy and despotism. In monarchy, the defining principle is honor. In despotism, it is a fear that "must beat down everyone's courage and extinguish even the slightest feeling of ambition." The contrast could not be sharper.

Law also plays a telling role within republics. Montesquieu was familiar with the Roman experience of republicanism; he had studied Machiavelli's *Discourses* and had written a (poorly received) book on Roman history. A republic, he explains, depends on the virtue of its people. There is therefore always a risk that an unvirtuous citizen will gather up for themselves exorbitant power, and the abuse of this power may well swing the polity toward something akin to despotism. The risk is all the greater because, unlike a monarchy, a republic may well not have laws to constrain the ensuing harms. This leads Montesquieu ultimately to a distinctive understanding of liberty as "the right to do everything the laws permit."

Law, then, plays an important role in the distinction between regimes where fear is dominant and regimes in which virtue and honor take center stage. Law plays this role by curbing the ability of a potential despot to exercise an unfettered will. It cultivates the "tranquility of spirit" that flows from knowing one need not fear one's fellow citizens. As in Locke's *Second Treatise*, the law is contrasted with arbitrariness. But Montesquieu's despotism is bleaker than anything Locke conjured. It is not just that property is insecure. It is a regime characterized by deep-rooted uncertainty about the law is one that stifles any economic or human flourishing, whether intimate, political, or economic, and in doing so immiserates all.

A second strand of the argument in *The Spirit of the Laws* concerns the structure of government. Among constitutional lawyers and scholars today, Montesquieu is celebrated for his idea of a separation of powers. He spun out this idea from observations of political life during a sojourn in England. His understanding of English constitutional arrangements was dubious, but his mistakes were generative. For Montesquieu, virtue, which is the principle of republics, is never sufficient to extinguish fear. Instead, he insists that checks on power must come though the "arrangement of things." Montesquieu asks how the very design of the state can be put to work in the service of liberty. His proposal, later taken up by the American constitutional architect James Madison, is that three separate functions of government can be distinguished and cleaved off from each other. These are the executive branch, the legislative branch, and the judiciary. For Montesquieu, the separation of judging from other functions is the pivot of liberty. So European states that combined the executive and the legislative remain free, while the Ottoman sultanate folded together all three into one institution, and so experienced an "atrocious despotism." The accuracy of this comparison is less important than the structural principle it purports to reveal. Yet Montesquieu was under no illusion that this sort of careful institutional design would be easy. Rather, combining and balancing powers required exquisite care. For all its horrors, despotic government is easier to fashion, and so more readily at hand.

In Montesquieu, then, we find variations on themes already sounded in Aristotle and Locke. Most importantly, there is the former's threefold taxonomy of regimes, and the intuition that law can play varying roles in different regimes. Montesquieu also echoes Locke's contrast between arbitrariness and legality. In

Montesquieu, the imprecise term "tyranny" is sharpened into a stark fear of being under the absolute mercy of another. Yet another echo of Locke's thought concerns the treatment of property. For both theorists, the rule of law is valuable precisely, and especially, because of the shield it offers to private property.

Magna Carta

Several historical documents in the Anglo-American legal tradition are also often identified as seeds for the rule of law. Among the most important of these is Magna Carta. The 1215 charter initially memorialized a deal between the English King John and his rebellious barons. Its 39th article appears to circumscribe a person's imprisonment or royal coercion "except by the lawful judgment of his equals or by the law of the land." That language, according to the late Justice Hugo Black of the US Supreme Court, is "the origin of due process."

But the matter is not so simple. To begin with, Magna Carta was just one of a long series of charters issued by the Angevin kings of England to advertise their virtues and promote peace in the land. Its limits on royal power were nothing new. They had long been thought implicit in the coronation oaths. The 1215 charter simply formalized widely shared unspoken understandings. It also did not work: by September 1215, most of the charter had proven a dead letter. The charter was then largely forgotten until the 1600s—a period of violent constitutional ferment in which the monarchy's authority was a central issue. Judges of that era, such as Edward Coke, offered a novel, largely false, version of English legal history. Coke mischaracterized rules flowing from the king (such as Magna Carta) or the royal courts as customary law that originated in the community. Writing in the 1760s, the influential jurist William Blackstone would follow Coke's lead and talk of "unchanged and unadulterated" laws that were as "old as the primitive Britons." Magna Carta came to be understood as part of this "ancient law." This was bad history, but it was immensely comforting at a moment when royal authority was in severe, even fatal, doubt.

In substance, moreover, Magna Carta was far from a triumph of law over sovereign power. It was, emphatically, a bargain struck by king and nobles meant to ensure their continued, profitable exploitation of the great majority of the feudal population. Nothing in Magna Carta suggested it had population-wide significance. There were no remedies available for its enforcement. Rather, it was a preeminently political document, a bargaining chip in future bickering between king and barons. Even Article 39's reading as the embryonic statement of due process and fair trial rights emerged only in the seventeenth century. These virtues were then read back into an imagined legal past.

All that said, the Magna Carta is today a potent symbol of law's power. In 2015 the Chinese government shuttered a planned public exhibition of a thirteenth-century copy of the charter, moving it from a publicly accessible location to the British ambassador's residence, with limited tickets. The Chinese characters for "Magna Carta" were also censored on Sina Weibo, China's main social-media platform. So perhaps it would be hasty to dismiss Magna Carta's significance to the rule of law. The historical Magna Carta may have had little effect. But an imagined Magna Carter, conjured first in England's tumultuous seventeenth century, continues to have a powerful grip on the imagination not just of Anglo-American lawyers, but also far afield.

Before the rule of law

None of the works of Aristotle, Locke, or Montesquieu contain the phrase "rule of law." Their key contribution was not a linguistic coinage. It was instead their probing explorations of ways in which law—by which they usually meant written law, especially legislation—can and should help build a decent society characterized by security and prosperity rather than fear.

At the core of this task, those three writers all perceived a central challenge. This was the need to distinguish passion (or arbitrariness) from reason (or law-based action) to elicit secure expectations and make both liberty and property possible. All three presented these distinctions as if they were transparent, needing no explanation. But we should pause before assuming that they were right to do so. How distinct, really, is our reason from our passions or our interests? What of passions such as compassion and mercy—are they just as corrupting as envy and fear? Should they too be purged from the law? And can we assume that merely because a law is written, and cast in a general form, that it reflects rationality at work? Further, are Montesquieu's anatomies of the articulated monarchy or the separation of powers persuasive? It is the power of these earlier writings to stimulate these questions, though, that makes them valuable and worth reading today. Like Kafka's literary precursors, they offer elements that can be assembled into something new and distinct—something that would later come to be called the rule of law.

Chapter 3
The rule of law's green shoots

The decades between 1850 and 1890 were a period of extraordinary change in the nature of the state. This was not just a matter of new states emerging in Germany and Italy. Cities such as London, St. Petersburg, and New York were in the process of quintupling in size. Dizzying increases in the production of coal, pig iron, and steel fed new railroads, navies, and armies. The railroad in turn enabled a new cadre of national leaders to wield authority over territories that had otherwise been a nation in name only. Many of the most powerful modern states were then in Europe. At the peripheries of their power, those states violently suppressed resistance to colonialism in Asia, Africa, and the Americas. These holdouts faced warships and Maxim guns, all deployed with ruthless and bloody determination. If the law was an answer to the problem of despotic state power, the basic terms of the question had dramatically changed. Could the ideal of legality keep up with these changes?

A case in point: In 1865 the British governor of Jamaica, Edward Eyre, invoked martial law to suppress a local uprising in Morant Bay. British troops shot and killed around 500 men, women, and children. Some were summarily executed. In London a group called the Jamaica Committee formed in response to bring private prosecutions against Eyre and his officers. As its chair, John Stuart Mill, would put it, their concern was not "only justice to the

Negros," but whether Great Britain itself was to be "under the government of law."

Among the members of this committee was a young lawyer and journalist, Albert Venn Dicey. Later in his career, Dicey would go on to write perhaps the most influential book on the rule of law published in the past 200 years. That work is not simply, or even principally, a response to his experience on the Jamaica Committee. Dicey was too rich, and too complex, a character for that. In 1911 Dicey still described himself as a committed "mid-Victorian." He was shaped decisively by Evangelical, Utilitarian, and Whig intellectual currents of his era. In his younger days, he wrote in favor of electoral reform and lamented his compatriots' support for slavery and the American Confederacy. But he was also a vehement opponent of home rule in Ireland. A profound trust in free markets and small government percolated through his works. For all that, the massacre of Morant Bay, whether or not it indeed haunted Dicey, offers a useful starting point for understanding why a set of lecture notes, designed to pull together undergraduate lessons on the general principles of English law, has become a starting point for much modern thinking about the rule of law. In particular, it offers a clue as to why Dicey came to see certain kinds of state power as a particularly stark and difficult problem.

The lectures arose from a professional obligation. In 1882 Dicey was appointed to the illustrious post of Vinerian chair of English law at Oxford University. His ensuing compilation of teaching materials, called *Lectures Introductory to the Study of the Law of Constitution*, set forth a new account of the English constitution as law. Of course, there was not then, and is not now, a compact written constitution in either Great Britain or England. Indeed, before Dicey the study of English law had been dominated by analytic, philosophical approaches and detailed historical studies. Dicey broke new ground by characterizing the constitution as law. It is not too much to say that for many lawyers his book *was* the constitution.

England's pride

Like Aristotle, Locke, and Montesquieu, Dicey did not set out to pen a volume on the rule of law. His topic was a description of the English constitution. Unlike Aristotle, Locke, and Montesquieu, however, he did use the phrase "rule of law." But he did so in service of a general description and justification of the English legal system, not with the ambition of any universal prescription.

In Dicey's telling, the English constitution rested on two bedrock principles: the sovereignty of Parliament and the rule of law. Expounding each of these general principles and explaining their relation were his book's core tasks. The first idea is simple enough. Parliament had an unlimited form of sovereignty, Dicey explained, in the sense of being competent to enact law on any topic. But it had to exercise its power to make or unmake law in a particular way—by enacting new legislation. This was, Dicey underscored, an "undoubted legal fact." What of the second idea? The specific phrase "rule of law" had been deployed here and there by earlier writers. Henry de Bracton and the classical republican theorist James Harrington had casually used it. Late nineteenth-century translators of Aristotle's *Politics*, indeed, used it with casual abandon. Earlier English legal thinkers, including Lord Mansfield, William Blackstone, and Jeremy Bentham, had debated the merits of anchoring legality in a thick account of English traditions and institutions, as opposed to emphasizing abstract qualities such as certainty and generality. But Dicey deserves credit for being the first to perceive a need to give the phrase a clear and distinct meaning. His definition has three distinct yet kindred moving parts. Plainly, they are intended to work together as a whole.

The first element of Dicey's rule of law speaks to the circumstances in which a person can properly be punished or made to suffer some personal loss or deprivation under the law. Dicey explained that neither should happen unless the fact of a legal breach is established "in the ordinary legal manner before the ordinary Courts of the land." This first plank of the rule of law binds all "persons in authority." And most of Dicey's examples hinge on officials who wielded the Crown's powers, not private power. Indeed, his principal example of how the law could fail along this dimension is drawn from the pre-revolutionary French monarchy of Montesquieu's era. The English, he posited, are distinct in having a shield from the arbitrary or unpredictable use of *state* power.

The second plank of Dicey's rule of law again concerns the courts. It demands that no one, whatever their rank or title, stand above the law. All must answer for their actions under the "ordinary law of the realm" and in the "ordinary" tribunals that handle all other matters. Again, France offered a counterexample; its administrative courts plucked lawsuits against officials out of the ordinary courts, subjecting them to a distinctive body of administrative law (*droit administratif*). Dicey labeled this a breach of "legal equality." The assumption driving Dicey's thought is plainly that specialized courts will give officials an easy ride. This would permit them more leeway to use their authority, even though this authority makes them a special danger to others. Dicey appeared not to have contemplated the possibility that officials' actions might raise legal questions with no parallel to the private conduct covered by ordinary law. For example, an official might be administering a comprehensive and mandatory health insurance scheme, of the sort created by German chancellor Otto von Bismarck in 1883, a system without historical or private analog at the time. Or consider a more contemporary example: What if officials have legal authority to conduct forms of electronic surveillance through wiretaps? These may be left unregulated by the ordinary law because they fall outside standard descriptions of tortious conduct. If so, a person subjected to unlawful state surveillance and then channeled into the ordinary courts would be without a remedy.

The third element of Dicey's rule of law concerns the origins of the constitution's "general principles." Unlike the US Constitution of 1787, the English one is made up of judicial decisions about the rights of private persons in respect to factual controversies. These "general principles" are not, to be clear, the same as "law." Dicey was quite explicit that he understood law to include the statutory handiwork of Parliament. The constitution's general principles, in contrast, are "judge made." They are generalizations, knitted out of arguments by judges in reported cases, or those statutes that "resemble" judicial decisions. To illustrate, Dicey offered the example of laws modifying and codifying a common-law remedy against executive detention called the writ of habeas corpus.

Today, the extraordinary global diffusion of written constitutions entrenched beyond casual legislative amendment gives Dicey's third argument a puzzling cast. Those habituated to the virtues of constitutional *kala grammata* (written rules) will find praise of its absence downright perverse. But Dicey had arguments for his seemingly eccentric position. For him, the judicial origin of general constitutional principles vouchsafed the constitution's organic, evolutionary quality. Perhaps this latter quality is valuable because a legal edifice built in increments is less vulnerable to erosion, or a decisive body blow, than one fashioned all at once. Dicey seemed to think so, but he did not persuasively explain why. An insistence on judicial incrementalism also reflects what Dicey imagined as a peculiar English insight—that a constitutional right is futile in the absence of a complementary remedy. He would have nodded in recognition at the plight of those whose constitutional rights are violated in the United States. In America the national Constitution largely lacks any detail about what remedies are available for constitutional violations. In practice, moreover, officials who do violate constitutional rights are rarely held liable in any subsequent legal action. For those at the greatest risk of police violence in particular, constitutional rights are often illusory. Thus, the Diceyan rule of law in modern America fails because of the weakness of constitutional remedies, a flaw that would have been immediately legible to the Victorian legal thinker.

These three principles place stress on the "ordinary" courts, applying "ordinary" law, as vessels by which the rule of law is realized. Dicey was acutely aware that this seems to be in tension with his commitment to parliamentary supremacy. He was careful nevertheless to reconcile these two pillars of English constitutionalism. The Crown in Parliament, he explained, can only act through Acts of Parliament. As he wrote in a letter to his friend and fellow scholar James Bryce, "The supremacy of the law has tended to increase the exercise of Parliamentary sovereignty." This means that the executive's actions are strictly defined by written law. Even in an emergency, Dicey explained, officials depend on either prior legislative authorization or an after-the-fact "indemnification" statute to bring their acts within the law. The parliamentary monopoly on lawmaking also empowers judges, who apply statutes by reference solely to the text of enacted law. This enlarges the "fixity of the law." As a result of mutual dependency, Parliament is zealous to protect the bench—hence its resistance to the blight of *droit administratif.* Parliamentary supremacy and the rule of law, in short, are not mutually antagonistic; they complement and enable each other. Working together, they generate an institutional division of powers—one that echoes in a way what Montesquieu termed the separation of powers.

What is Dicey's rule of law worth?

Dicey has been criticized as boorishly parochial and xenophobic. Certainly, he had no excess of affection for the French. But his project was never universal in character. He set out to map English constitutional law as a field of inquiry. He thus meant to explain how the rule of law was realized *in England.* Dicey was willing to recognize that other constitutions did a reasonable job of advancing liberty under the rule of law. (Not France, of course—but Belgium!) Other legal traditions developed concepts close, if not identical, to the rule of law. Perhaps the most important parallel tradition was created by German jurists of the nineteenth and early twentieth centuries, beginning with Robert von Mohl. They explored and celebrated versions of what they called *Rechtsstaat* (roughly, the "constitutional state"), which linked the legitimacy of the state to the constant exercise of its power through law. The *Rechtsstaat* tradition thus covers similar terrain to the rule-of-law tradition, but diverges in its focus. Perhaps it would be wrong then to say that Dicey's three general principles were the only means of expressing the rule of law in practice, or the only way of benchmarking the actual law against an ideal. But it would also be wrong to dismiss out of hand his idea that they could be *a* way of doing so.

A better way of approaching Dicey's three principles is to reflect on how they might apply in practice. A contemporary application of those principles to a variant on the scenario of Morant Bay is one way to do this. In 1867 the British Government of India passed "An Act for the Suppression of Murderous Outrages in Certain Districts of the Punjab." This targeted a group labeled "fanatics," who plotted or attempted assaults on imperial servants. "Fanatics" were denied rights ordinarily available in criminal trials, such as the right to legal counsel, the right to appeal a conviction, and the benefit of formal rules of evidence. They could be detained for any length of time. The presiding authority could decide to examine witnesses—or not. He could sentence a fanatic to immediate execution and order the disposal of the body as he saw fit—most often by burning. The legal regime created by this statute elicited practices—the public hanging of the living and the grotesque dissection of the dead—long abandoned in Dicey's Oxford.

What would Dicey have said? Despite joining the Jamaica Committee, he was an ardent imperialist. Without irony, he proclaimed confidently that "European notions of fairness and humanity" more than justified British rule over the territories. But he was also capable of nuanced judgments. Despite his fierce opposition to Irish Home Rule, Dicey was a vocal critic of the lawless and cruel treatment of certain Irish nationalists. So we cannot rule him out as a source of insight based on his attitudes about empire alone.

At first blush, the Murderous Outrages Act seems squarely at odds with Dicey's rule of law. It applies an extraordinary body of law to a disfavored group. This seems at odds with his first principle. The ordinary procedural frame of adjudication is wrenched apart. No regard is paid to "general principles" of law—including the remedy of habeas corpus. On the other hand, it is not clear that the act derogates from the "ordinary" rules of criminal justice in British India. Provided the act defined the crimes of a "fanatic," and enumerated clearly the punishments that followed, why should it not be counted as just another swatch of the "ordinary" law fit for imperial purpose? Nor is it clear that the officials who resolved cases under the act could not count as "courts." In another book, Dicey defined a court as a body that resolved disputes not in terms of fairness but in accord with "some definite principle of law." It is far from clear that this criterion was violated under the act. Consider further that a descendant of the Murderous Outrages Act remains the law today in Pakistan, 150 years later, in the form of the Frontier Crimes Regulation. In force for more than a century and a half, why should it be denied the status of "ordinary law" ready to be applied by "ordinary courts"?

Further, the act could be said to comply with Dicey's second principle because it created no special privileges for officials. And if the act was the product of an appropriate legislative process, surely it vindicated the principle of parliamentary supremacy. More generally, if the legislature in its sovereign capacity decided that a class of persons presented so grave a danger that they had to be met with abbreviated processes, then surely parliamentary supremacy and a strict fidelity to the text of the act meant that judges had no choice but to permit fanatics to be hanged, flayed, and desecrated. In any case, Dicey gives no reason to think that a court could look to "constitutional principles," or anything else so woolly, to deny force to the words of a duly enacted statute. In a pinch, conflict between parliamentary sovereignty and the rule of law could reemerge. Most of Dicey's arguments point toward the victory of law's letter over legality as principle if that happens. Indeed, his reaction was muted when the English courts upheld detentions under vague and broad language in the 1914 Defense of the Realm Act "for securing the public safety and the defense of the realm." He expressed "regret," but did not condemn the judges for going awry.

Much depends, in short, on the quality of Dicey's "ordinary law" and "ordinary courts," as well as the moral fiber of parliamentarians. His rule of law has varying consequences, then, as the background quality of institutions, judges, and legislators evolves.

Dicey's lessons for the rule of law

Dicey's argument is a first concrete step in a longer tradition of reflecting on the rule of law as an explicitly theorized concept. There is both innovation and continuity in his approach. On the one hand, Dicey echoed in important ways Aristotle's resistance to unruly passions, Locke's aversion to arbitrary action, and Montesquieu's hostility to despotism. On the other, his celebration of unspoken yet binding constitutional principle lacked a harbinger in Aristotle, Locke, or Montesquieu.

Where Dicey tracks earlier writers, however, he also abraded their arguments to a finer point. Echoing Locke, he brought a sharp focus on arbitrary or despotic action by the state. In his hands, the rule of law becomes a tool for managing the risk of officials' abuse of their power. Dicey nowhere defends his focus on the state. But the secular acceleration in coercive state capacity during his lifetime provides a powerful justification for his focus. Despotism might still exist in the domestic sphere—a theme of Montesquieu's *Persian Letters*—but its public forms become more pressing as the state expands by leaps and bounds. Further, application of the rule of law to the state might be a necessary step for realizing protection against private despotisms. That is, unless the state is first disciplined by law, it is unlikely to be an ally against concentrations of private power wielded in arbitrary and harmful ways.

Dicey can be pressed further on this point. It is not just that the state is a distinctive object of moral concern. It is that there are specific elements, or functions, of the state that trigger sharp worries. Dicey's "general principles" of constitutional law, such as the right of "personal liberty" and the right of "public meeting," suggest as much. He underscored that these rights persist even when riot or invasion requires military action. His principles, indeed, anticipate those found in the 1966 International Covenant on Civil and Political Rights. The latter are generally directed, in the first instance at least, against the coercive might of the state. There is a logic to this. If the state can use its control over the means of legitimate violence to cow people, the shadow of physical violence undermines their interests in many other contexts where the state is not involved. Freedom from arbitrary state violence has a primal quality.

Yet there is also a strand of Dicey's writing that takes a bigger tranche of state activity as objectionable on rule-of-law grounds. In a subsequent book, he railed against the "collectivism" of the early British welfare state. Ivor Jennings, a leading constitutional expert of mid-twentieth-century Britain, dismissed Dicey's work as a subconscious reaction to the intervention of the state in the economy. Dicey, said Jennings, "wanted nothing which interfered with profits, even if profits involved child labor, wholesale factory accidents, the pollution of rivers, of the air, and the water-supply." As the idea of the rule of law was to develop over the twentieth century, Dicey's wider angle on what counts as worrisome state activity would be taken up by different thinkers.

Dicey made further progress by offering a new sketch of institutional distinctions upon which to base the rule of law. This echoed Montesquieu's separation of powers. But its specific grammar is new. Dicey's account was centered on the mutual dependence between parliamentary sovereignty and a court-centered understanding of legality, organized around "general principles" that emerge organically out of the mass of case law. The last element contrasts starkly with Aristotle's and Locke's insistence upon written, legislated law. Unlike them, Dicey's argument placed load-bearing weight on the judiciary. He assumed judges are categorically different from other officials in how they respond to legal sources, but did not provide evidence for this assumption. It is an open question whether this view accurately describes the English courts in Dicey's time. Their approach to the Defense of the Realm Act does not foster optimism on this score. Dicey's theory also assumes well-functioning "ordinary" courts and legislative processes. But he does not offer a sufficient explanation of how such well-ordered institutions come about in the first place, and then continue to work reasonably well in moments of stress. It is here that the criticisms of Dicey's Little Englishness may have the most purchase. His telling of the rule of law might reflect a regrettable, even smug, complacency about the availability and endurance of high-quality institutions.

Further, Dicey assumed that good courts and legislators are sufficient to create the rule of law. But imagine a place where courthouses are ringed by armed soldiers, who prevent a regime's enemies from ever filing a case. Or imagine a place where courts charge filing fees that elevate litigation beyond the economic means of a majority. Or a place where racial animus means that members of a discrete minority are consistently treated with disabling contempt by judicial officials. These examples suggest that Dicey's rule of law depends not just on institutions, but also on the quality of the larger society. Yet if the rule of law turns on the larger pattern of society, as these examples suggest, what would be distinctively *legal* about the rule of law?

Dicey's legacy

Had he merely been the first to use the phrase "rule of law" in a systematic way, Dicey's posterity would have been assured. But his contribution to the rule of law is greater. His understanding of its distinctive relation to the state, its capacity to enable basic negative rights, and its institutional anchor in the judiciary all persist to this day. Nevertheless, Dicey's was not the last word on the rule of law. To the contrary, his was the opening chord of a symphony that was to ebb and then crescendo across the long and bloody twentieth century.

Chapter 4
Three branches of the modern rule of law

To live at the end of the twentieth century, for many Americans, was to be beset by very public doubts about the rule of law. A tight presidential race in November 2000 hung on the outcome of protracted recounts in Florida. When a majority of the US Supreme Court—all appointed by Republican presidents—cut short those tallies to the benefit of Republican candidate George W. Bush, many cried foul. Writing in dissent in *Bush v. Gore*, Justice John Paul Stevens captured their concerns when he bemoaned the majority decision as a blow to "the Nation's confidence in the judge as an impartial guardian of the rule of law." *Bush v. Gore* is not the only high court intervention to attract criticism on rule-of-law grounds. In the United Kingdom, the Supreme Court's ruling on Prime Minister Boris Johnson's prorogation of Parliament faced the same sort of criticism. The Tory politician Jacob Rees-Mogg characterized it as a "constitutional coup" at odds with the rule of law. Courts, which Dicey had celebrated as cornerstones of the rule of law, suddenly were condemned as its enemy. Something in the public understanding of the rule of law has plainly drifted from its initial moorings.

Dicey's depiction of the English rule of law as three general principles proved, indeed, a seed for a vivid flowering of varying ideas about the rule of law. Perhaps because it had so much productive ambiguity, it proved especially fertile ground for those wishing to make fresh demands of the law. The resulting profusion of "rules of law" has provoked much skepticism. At one point, the American political theorist Judith Shklar queried (a bit theatrically) whether it was all "ruling class chatter."

To answer Shklar's question, we need some way to organize the main lines of development of rule-of-law ideas in the twentieth century. This is no straightforward task. Books and papers on the rule of law, many proposing their own novel versions of it, could fill a library wing. Some scholars insist there is only one way of defining that term. Others offer a variety of taxonomies. Any classification system is going to be controversial, for any serious effort at a taxonomy needs to make judgments about how to group, prioritize, and evaluate ideas. This one is no different.

That said, there are three main lines or branches of twentieth-century thinking about the rule of law. Each of these three branches appeals to a different set of values. Each one corresponds to a different ambition for the law. Each distinct ambition can be aligned for the sake of exposition with a different academic discipline, because each one can be said to bring its own priorities to bear in thinking about the rule of law. The three branches are thus labeled here after the three main disciplines that study legal systems. They are the lawyer's, the political philosopher's, and the economist's rule of law. Use of these labels does not mean that only lawyers, or all lawyers, line up behind the first of these versions of the rule of law. Far from it.

One of the most important arguments for the lawyer's version of the rule of law was made by an Oxford philosopher Joseph Raz. But he appeals to values of interest to lawyers. Its cornerstone is efficacy. The second branch is concerned with a wider array of goods that law might elicit for people at large. It evaluates the law in terms of a broader vision of a just society. This is a value studied most closely by political philosophers. The final branch of rule-of-law thinking draws attention to the relation between the law and the economy. It is concerned with the contribution that legal institutions make to the operation of the free market. This economist's view of the rule of law is, like the political philosopher's, a vision of what law contributes to a larger social project. But the two accounts are different in scope and consequence because of their distinct ethical ambitions for society.

Like wandering tributaries of a great river, these three versions of the rule of law blend and drift apart. They nevertheless answer slightly different questions. The lawyer's telling is concerned with "how" law works, while the political philosopher's and the economist's versions explain "why" the rule of law is desirable. So the rule of law can be understood in terms of means or ends. From yet another angle, it might be said that the rule of law, in all its forms, is tied to the political project of liberalism. This is helpful so far as it goes. But it goes only a short way. The Cambridge philosopher Raymond Geuss once drily remarked that the term "liberalism" could be used to as a general catch-all to describe almost every position taken in the Western tradition of political philosophy. So it is with the rule of law. Indeed, even traditions that eschew the liberal label have use of the rule of law.

How to make law work for you

Imagine you are a ruler—whether king, prime minister, or president—and you wish to use law as a tool for creating social order. You may be moved by a benevolent desire to create a peaceful, well-ordered society for citizens. Or perhaps it is simply too tiresome and expensive to keep your secret police and jackbooted thugs ready to go all the time. Even torturers need a day off. The decision to use law as a technology of rule can have many motivating springs. But having decided to use the law to rule, it is necessary to identify those characteristics of law that make it effective. Law does its work only if it can guide those under its canopy. One version of the rule of law, the lawyer's version, picks out the qualities of law necessary for it to fulfill this guidance function. So this rule of law is a necessary condition of law's efficacy. Its long suit, indeed, is that it is difficult to see how law can work as a tool for even minimal social organization unless its preconditions are satisfied. Its weak suit is that it is hard to know what else cuts in its favor.

An efficacy-based understanding of the rule of law turns on the capacity of legal rules to offer guidance. This has several implications. Legal rules, whether embodied in statutes, constitutions, or judicial decisions, must be clear. They must be promulgated to the public and written in a way most people can comprehend. They also must be consistent and stable. They cannot careen wildly from one context to another or from one instant to another. It also helps popular compliance if the laws are general in scope and do not go about their business by picking out this or that person for particularized demands. In addition, the law must not be retroactive. Since people can only make decisions about what they will do in the future, it is futile, as well as cruel, to instruct them on what they needed to do in the past. This last point can be generalized out a bit more: laws must be capable of being obeyed. They must not ask the impossible of their subjects. It follows that the laws on the books must in fact be enforced by officials charged with making the law stick. Where that congruence between letter and action is lacking, all the other qualities of the rule of law are likely futile.

A list of this sort, tailored to the project of enabling the law to guide behavior, has been offered by several Anglo-American legal scholars. The best known are those penned by the Harvard law professor Lon Fuller (who wrote of "legality" rather than the "rule of law") and the English scholars Joseph Raz and John Finnis. Theirs is sometimes called a "formal" understanding of the rule of law. But this terminology may be misleading. The prohibitions on retroactive law and opaque law, for example, could be said to do more than just regulate the "form" of law. They also forbid certain kinds of substantive regulation of people's conduct. So the term "formal," although commonly used, is best avoided.

Instead, the lawyer's version of the rule of law is concerned with the proper modalities of legal rules. Except for its last element, it can be tested by examining the law on the books. So it has relatively little to say about how legal institutions ought to operate. It does not play favorites between courts, bureaucracies, or even inquisitors—so long as they are in the business of applying the law as written. This is a weakness as well as a strength.

Like Dicey's, the lawyer's version implicitly makes quite demanding assumptions about its broader social and institutional context. Not least, it requires that legal institutions, and especially courts, be open and generally available to resolve disputes. If many people lack the material resources to hire lawyers, this kind of rule of law will also have little practical bite. Even in wealthy countries, the absence of state-funded legal aid or high levels of illiteracy (say, among the prison populace) places the law out of the reach for many people. Some rule-of-law theorists, such as Joseph Raz, pay close attention to these assumed capabilities. Worry about them led Raz to deny that the rule of law is a "universal standard of justice." It is, instead, at best a touchstone in societies with the necessary material, institutional, and cultural resources. Yet other thinkers have suggested that the lawyers' theory of the rule of law needs to be complemented with a comprehensive explanation of what makes legal institutions just in order to be morally appealing.

At times, some of the elements of the lawyer's rule of law are pushed to an extreme. The American jurist Antonin Scalia, for example, strictly favored "clear and definite" rules over mushy all-things-considered "standards" on rule-of-law grounds. This would, for example, select for a "drive no more than 50 miles-per-hour" rule over a "drive reasonably" standard. Vague standards, Scalia's argument goes, leave too much discretion in the hands of judges and other officials. So they offend against the rule of law. There is plainly something to this. But it is risky to make too much of it. It is often impossible and undesirable to eliminate all vagueness from the law. Consider the law of fraud or tax evasion. A community that limited itself to a list of impermissible frauds and tax dodges would empower the scofflaw. In a democratic regime with a functioning legislative branch, moreover, statutes will often be a product of wheeling, dealing, and ugly compromise. It is quite likely that this sort of eminently desirable deliberation on public policy will often lead to textual fudges. A legal system that cannot deal with such ambiguity is not well-equipped for the real world of democratic politics.

Indeed, all the rule-of-law traits valued in the lawyer's version are matters of degree. None is plausibly treated as an absolute quality that is simply either present or absent. This is because no legal system does, or could, pursue any one of these qualities to a logical limit. Both life and parliamentary sessions are too short to develop utterly clear statutory text. Lawmakers cannot predict all possible situations the future might throw up, and so they necessarily write down what prove in the end to be ambiguous statutes.

Some of the demands made by the lawyer's rule of law, moreover, risk counterproductive effects. Take the idea of public accessibility. A law that is kept secret from the public is not one that can provide guidance. Yet, in practice, this seems to matter little. Very few people know what the law requires. Even lawyers must often consult a treatise or a statute book to find out what the law is. Taken very seriously, an accessibility rule might require that laws be drafted in ways that are readily comprehensible to all the regulated population. But a demand for simplicity along these lines could well make law less precise. It would likely enable more open-ended discretion by officials.

Further, there may well be times when keeping certain elements of the law secret is a positive good. Imagine, for example, that criminal prosecutors permit a "battered spouse's defense" in domestic violence cases. The prosecutors could reasonably conclude that having such a defense is compassionate and wise, but it also risks encouraging some violence that could be avoided. Ideally, the law would make this defense available, but also conceal that fact from the general public. Likewise, a legal regime that eschewed all retroactivity would turn its face on any new law that changed the ongoing practical significance of a past action. But at the same time, this would be paralyzing. In practice, many new rules that apply only after a law's enactment can alter the expected value of past investments. A town subject to an absolute prospectivity regime, as a result, could never change its property tax or land-use regimes without dramatically changing the expected values of existing real property investments. But it would still experience unexpected bouts of economic growth, environmental problems, or even pandemics. These nonlegal shocks would alter the practical effects of existing land-use rules even without any formal change in the law. So why should legal shocks be thought of any differently from other external forces that change valuations? As a character in Giuseppe Tomasi di Lampedusa's novel, *The Leopard*, explains, "for things to remain the same, everything must change." This may well be true too for law.

The lawyer's rule of law, in other words, is best taken as a "general principle" of the kind Dicey celebrated. It is to be doled out with scrupulous care and moderation, keeping in mind the actual quiddities and foibles not just of a legal system but also of real people. A slavish devotion to precise compliance is a grave error that may well make the law seem foolish, or even cruel.

The efficacy-oriented understanding of the rule of law runs into three worries. First, it assumes that the goal of lawmakers is to guide their subjects. But is this always so? Consider one of the world's first great law codes, the 282 Babylonian laws from the early eighteenth century BCE now dubbed the Code of

Hammurabi. These rules were, in practice, not followed in actual disputes. Modern students of early Mesopotamian cultures have come to understand the code less as a statute book and more as a hortatory expression of the duties and limits of royal power. Many well-known clauses of modern constitutions have the same function. For example, the Hungarian and Chinese constitutions pledge fealty to the rule of law. The US Constitution's commitments to a "republican form of government" and "equal protection" in practice hover at a dignified remove from the actual facts of US society. Law, in short, can have several functions. Guidance need not dominate.

A second worry about this account of the rule of law focuses on its assumptions about what makes law capable of offering guidance. Dicey associated the rule of law with the courts. He celebrated how "general principles" of law emerged piecemeal in long chains of decided cases. This contrasted favorably for him with European efforts to distill law down to a code, from which results could then be neatly deduced. But the lawyer's version of the rule of law described here is in tension with Dicey's vision. If constitutional principles, or any law, emerge piecemeal across many cases, they are not going to be timely promulgated or clearly stated up front. Dicey's court-centered perspective, that is, appears to flout the rule of law's guidance function.

How are these pressures to be resolved? Dicey suggested that judge-made law can offer guidance as much as legislation can if it meets a different set of criteria. He underscored the importance of respecting earlier decisions, or precedent, as a means of generating disciplined and stable law. Consistent with this view, the Anglo-American legal tradition suggests that law need not be clear, promulgated, or stable in order to offer guidance. There are many principles, and even specific rules, of law that have emerged organically through a long series of cases. In the law of personal wrongs, or torts, for example, many cases are governed by a principle of negligence. This idea, which originated in the courts, and not a legislature, imposes a duty of reasonable care to avoid harms. It might be thought that the term "reasonable care" is excessively vague. In fact, it seems to provide sufficient guidance to enable good enough planning. Indeed, precisely because it is so vague, the "reasonable care" standard can be applied across a broad swath of human life. It works as a single, tolerably clear legal norm that takes the place of countless micro-rules, each tailored to a specific kind of human activity.

Finally, it is important to ask whether the rule of law, understood in these terms, is worthy of great moral praise. The American jurist Lon Fuller asserted that this rule of law was in effect an "internal morality" of a legal system that effectively curbed certain abuses of power. Fuller thought that certain sorts of infamous regimes, such as Nazism, could not get off the ground without jettisoning this internal morality. This seems rather doubtful. The law, for example, played an important role in maintaining slavery in both Europe and the Americas through the nineteenth century. It offered the designers of the Jim Crow regime in the post–Civil War US South a crucial set of tools. And it has been an important part of the processes whereby women have been denied economic and political freedoms, and even the autonomy of making choices about their own bodies, in countless different cultures and times. But Fuller may well be correct in a more limited way to the extent that there are certain kinds of barbarity that cannot easily be accommodated within this rule of law. Between 1966 and 1969, for example, Mao Zedong fomented an internal rebellion by young Red Guard cadres within the Chinese Communist party-state. By 1967 the civilian state had largely collapsed. Violent conflict quickly spread around the country. This Cultural Revolution, as it came to be known, claimed the lives of some 1.6 million people until it ran out of steam. Fuller is probably right that a violent anarchy akin to the Cultural Revolution cannot occur within the rule of law. But he is wrong to suggest that the lawyer's idealized version of the rule of law offers adequate protection against all (or more) of the worst that humanity has to offer.

More modestly, it might be said that this version of the rule of law, in its ruthless quest for efficacy, at least treats its subjects as rational autonomous beings. It does this, however, by assuming a knowledge of the law, and a capacity to navigate it, far beyond what most people possess. Yet its implausible model of human rationality is evidence not of its failure, but of the zeal with which it advances the interests of the governing over the governed.

How law can advance justice

The chilly moral agnosticism of the lawyer's rule of law invites a more robust telling of the rule of law. This one would focus not just on the "how" but also explicitly on the "why" of law. If the law is to be held to an aspirational standard, that is, should it not be an illustrious and noble one? If the best the law can be is functional, then the rule of law's moral value dwindles dramatically. It also loses contact with how lay people understand it. Ask a person on the street if the law exists when a Stasi officer can arrest anyone at night, when secret prisons house torture cells and rape rooms, or when morality police ruthlessly beat to death women with insufficient hair covering—all of which were consistent with the then applicable laws on the books. The lawyer's understanding of rule of law, in other words, stands at a discordant distance from everyone else's.

One response to the seemingly impoverished moral ambitions of the lawyer's rule of law is to couple the concept more explicitly to some set of cherished substantive individual rights. A legal system can be said to conform to the rule of law on this view not only when it guides people's conduct effectively, but also when it advances certain foundational human interests. Law is valuable because it enables human flourishing. Given the orientation of this line of thought, it is usefully labeled the political philosopher's rule of law. It invests law with the promise of creating a just social order—a concept of core concern to political philosophers. That is, it goes far beyond just a functioning cluster of legal institutions. Rather than efficacy, its touchstone is a loftier goal of justice.

There are several justice-oriented views of the rule of law. Some are to be found in the work of political philosophers such as John Rawls and Ronald Dworkin. Perhaps the most influential such argument, however, was offered by a working judge rather than by a philosopher. Lord Tom Bingham of the United Kingdom's House of Lords was, prior to his death in 2010, a member of the apex tribunal for that nation. Bingham's book *The Rule of Law* has been influential not just because of his position as a judge, but also because it is unusually lucid and readily grasped. It is usefully taken as a paradigm of a justice-oriented account of the rule of law.

To begin with, Bingham is clear that his explanation of the rule of law supplements the lawyer's rule of law, rather than replacing it. It starts from the premise that the rules of a legal system ought to be public, general in scope, prospective, and possible to obey. This, however, is a floor and not a ceiling. History, starting from Magna Carta and culminating in the international treaties of human rights and humanitarian practice in wartime, warns against too chary an approach to the rule of law. We can also ask that the law leash public officials so they remain within its bounds, and so exercise their tremendous power in good faith for the public's benefit. The law can also guarantee a host of rights recognized by all as "fundamental." Consistent with the rule of law, the state cannot take life absent extraordinary circumstances. It cannot countenance torture. It abhors slavery. It advances rights to privacy, to family, to religious conscience, to free speech and free association, and to the freedom to marry. Trials must be prompt and fair. The larger international legal order receives its due regard.

There is, without question, much that likely appeals to many in this robust and extensive understanding of the rule of law.

Bingham's treatment of the rule of law is what Ronald Dworkin calls a "rights conception." But there are also two reasons for hesitation in respect to Bingham's approach. The first turns on the substantive rights that the rule of law protects. Bingham asserts that there is a class of rights and freedom that are "seen" as "fundamental." Alas, the use of a passive construction here obscures a difficulty. There is in practice rather wide disagreement about what counts as a foundational right. In the United States, to take an extreme example, the term is likely to conjure quite different lists from different people. Some might list the right to be free of structural racism or sexism and the right to define one's own sexual identity and make one's own reproductive choices. Others might point to the right to carry a firearm and to act on their religious preferences even if this means seriously harming someone else. In the United Kingdom, Conservative governments periodically promise to repeal the 1998 Human Rights Act, which enshrines into statutory law many rights and freedoms that Bingham celebrates. Just as on the western side of the Atlantic, it is difficult to see a political consensus on fundamental rights. The political philosopher's recounting of the rule of law cannot rely on what is "seen" by everyone as "fundamental." There is simply too much disharmony for that. Instead, it needs to make a choice about what counts as fundamental. In order to do so, however, it cannot just rely on a story of how a legal system works, or what it means for law to play a guidance function. Instead, it must paint a broader portrait of a just society. This is a big task. It will not yield agreement either. People everywhere disagree on what justice looks like. If anything, this sort of disagreement is on the rise in the early twenty-first century. So the political philosopher's rule of law is stuck between seemingly interminable social conflict and the shortcut of simply instructing people peremptorily on the basic terms of a just society. Neither path seems terribly appealing.

A second worry is related to the scope of this version of the rule of law. It is commonly thought that the rule of law is about, well, law. The political philosopher's model, however, hitches it to a broader conception of a just society. In this way, it could be said to turn the rule of law from one value among many into a comprehensive social theory. But a society might be committed to other values, such as democratic self-rule, restitution for past mass injustices, or a robust social safety net. There might be conflict between legality and other goals. Too capacious an understanding of the rule of law may mislead people into believing that they do not need to make hard choices between these ends. This mistake may further have perverse consequences. It is natural, following Dicey, to think that the rule of law demands the submission of all questions of law to a court. So the political philosopher's view of the rule of law may point toward the need for a court with broad competence to settle matters of justice. In practice, however, this may invite severe problems. In many societies, the bench and bar are generally drawn from wealthy, high-status ranks of society. They are unlikely to reflect the full range of interests of both rich and poor, and yet are more likely to believe themselves in possession of special political wisdom. A political system that submits legislation to broad judicial review risks the creation of an elite censor on democratic efforts to advance a inclusive, egalitarian, and just society. The American case lends sustenance to these worries. Judicial review in the United States has had generally regressive consequences for most of American history. Despite a judicial oath that requires judges to do "equal right to the poor and to the rich," the skew of American constitutionalism has been sharply regressive rather than even-handed thanks to the central role that an elite and elistist judiciary has played in its developed.

How the law can promote efficiency

The political philosophers' recounting of the rule of law is ambitious. It promises a just society as a downstream benefit of a legal system. It is possible, however, to tell a story about the legal system as a benefit to society that has a less ambitious footprint. One influential summary of the rule of law does just this by focusing on the relationship between the legal system and the free market for goods and services. The rule of law, this view contends, is to be embraced because it ensures the sound operation of that free market. The latter, in turn, has a distinctive capability for aggregating information about people's potential contributions, desires, and needs. A free market can take advantage of dispersed information to generate a desirable allocation of goods and services without arbitrary or coercive interventions. The market contrasts starkly, in this regard, with a centrally planned state. The benefits of the rule of law center on freedom from arbitrary state interventions that necessarily follow from an abandonment of the free market. It is appropriate to call this an economist's view of the rule of law because the market is the core object of contemporary economists' study. In much modern economics, the market is also invested with moral significance as a desirable mechanism for allocating resources to achieve productive efficiency. That is, the market allocates resources to their maximally productive use, thus increasing net productivity, and hence the overall wealth, of a society. By facilitating this process, the economist's rule of law enables what is perceived as a social good via a quite specific transactional mechanism.

The kernel of this argument was first developed by the Viennese-born economist Friedrich Hayek. Teaching at the London School of Economics in the early 1930s, Hayek saw the first budding hints of the British welfare state as the beginnings of a dangerous drift toward a brand of fascism that had poisoned Germany. Alarmed, he penned a cautionary note to the head of his institution, Sir William Beveridge, warning against the creation of new government services. The note did not work as intended. To the contrary, Beveridge would go on to write a report in 1942 on "Social Insurance and Allied Services," which would serve as the intellectual foundation of the postwar British welfare state. If Hayek lost the battle, however, he was determined to prevail in the broader war for hearts and minds. His note became a 1944 book, written for a broad popular audience, called *The Road to Serfdom*.

The ideas in that early work were further developed in a 1960 volume, *The Constitution of Freedom*. This was followed by a three-volume work titled *Law, Legislation, and Liberty*, published between 1973 and 1979. The first two of these three volumes offer arguments for how the rule of law can be understood as a commitment to free markets. The third refines that argument by chiseling out a preference for the body of judge-made law, which is called the "common law" in Anglo-American legal cultures, over legislation.

Legend has it that the Conservative politician Margaret Thatcher, before she became Britain's prime minister, had a habit of pulling *The Constitution of Liberty* from her handbag and declaring, "This is what we believe in!" Put aside the awkwardness of this story (Hayek's postscript to that book is titled "Why I Am Not a Conservative.") A consequence of its staying power has been that Hayek is read now in light of policies that Thatcher and similar political leaders pursued. To understand the economist's rule of law, however, it is worth stepping back to consider Hayek's arguments on their own terms, rather than reading them simply as forerunners of what would later be called "neoliberalism" or the "Washington Consensus." The earlier arguments of *The Road to Serfdom* and *The Constitution of Freedom* are a good place to start.

The core of Hayek's argument for the rule of law starts with its antithesis: the Nazi state that dominated Germany from 1933 onward. The force that dragged the Germans into fascism, posits Hayek, was socialism. Germans rejected the basic liberal principle that as much as possible of a society's ordering should be spontaneous and as little as possible should be coerced. Impatient with this principle, Germans on both the left and the right had insisted instead that state planning should oust the "impersonal and spontaneous" operation of the market. But this ouster of the market, argued Hayek, led directly and precipitously to a disastrous loss of individual liberties. Germans had lost sight of the way in which the knowledge of dispersed individuals can be aggregated into information in the form of price signals and came to believe instead that the state, through central planning, could achieve the same effect. This was a mistake. They forgot that the genius of the market was its capacity to concentrate information into a single variable—prices—and so enable all to instantaneously adapt themselves to the needs of others. In contrast, central planning demands a countless series of choices about how resources are allocated and who receives what. Planners, though, have no morally defensible way of making these choices. The result is a necessarily arbitrary and coercive pattern of interventions against individuals. This, urged Hayek, in a partial echo of Locke and Montesquieu, "leads straight to the totalitarian state."

Observance of the rule of law checks this slide into despotism. Simply put, the rule of law arises on Hayek's account when all state action is channeled through fixed and known rules that make it predictable. In large measure, this means honoring the lawyer's rule of law: binding law must be public, stable, and general. As Dicey instructed, penalties can be imposed only if an existing law is violated. Discretion must be subject to careful, after-the-fact review. Known and stable law, moreover, must also be fashioned well before the moment of its application. A break in time between the creation of law and its application makes that law impersonal, and so impartial.

But such "procedural" constraints, as Hayek called them, are never enough to realize the rule of law. The rule of law also needs to oust all measures that are incompatible with a "free system." This system is one in which people can plan their economic activities with certainty in advance. The rule of law precludes, as a matter of definition, all forms of central planning, such as the fixing of prices, quantities, or other terms of sale. It forbids state control of entry to different trades. And above all it rules out all state efforts at distributive justice; it is inconsistent with any effort to ensure that people are compensated according to merit or desert, as opposed to the "value that their services have for their fellows." Central planning can never come close to the rule of law because it demands that the state engage in an endless stream of ad hoc, arbitrary decisions. It starts with the introduction of vague language into legislation and inevitably ends with a regime in which decisions are taken based on status. Economic motives pervade both public and private spheres. A central planner, therefore, will find it irresistible to regulate the "whole of our lives"—from work, to leisure, to our friends, to our family.

A touchstone of Hayek's argument for the rule of law is thus a certain sort of liberty. This is understood solely in relation to the state. In contrast, the modern economist's idea of efficiency has a less significant role. The preferred form of liberty, Hayek freely conceded, is compatible with enormous disparities in wealth. Contrary to his contemporary reputation, however, he is not entirely insensitive to the plight of the poor. He was willing to countenance measures such as a basic income, social insurance, and even macroeconomic interventions to head off "large-scale unemployment." These measures, he thought, can be accomplished without excessively bruising the rule of law through the use of general, fixed, and predictable rules. Nor indeed was he entirely adverse to a regulatory state. To the contrary, Hayek chastised Dicey for his blinkered contempt for French administrative law tools that can offer more effective oversight than ordinary courts. Somewhat ironically, in his later work in the 1970s, Hayek shifted toward a vision closer to Dicey's. He insisted that the rule of law could only be advanced by exclusive reliance on the common law, through which unspoken yet pervasive principles of social ordering could emerge organically. At the same time, he anathematized legislation.

Hayek's arguments for a rule of law tightly connected to the free market have, no doubt, been extremely influential. But his vision is amenable to several powerful responses. A first objection concerns Hayek's telling of historical dynamics. His argument from history rests upon an implausible and selective view of the rise of interwar fascism in European countries. Indeed, it is simply wrong. Fascist parties emerged in several countries, but did not always prevail as in Italy and Germany. Across the board, they rose to prominence by forging alliances with conservative and rural factions, while also opposing themselves to urban socialist parties. But once within the political system, neither Mussolini nor Hitler achieved comprehensive political power through a free and fair election. In both countries, it was the conservative establishment that brought them into office without the imprimatur of an electoral victory supported by a majority of the voting public. By contrast, in Romania and Austria, fascist movements were quickly suppressed by the conservative establishment. Plainly, it is not socialism, but conservative elites, who bear blame for what followed. Hayek's history is clouded by a troubling opportunism that seeks to make moral capital out of the tragedy of interwar fascisms.

Subsequent events have been no kinder to Hayek's claim that there is an inexorable slippery slope from price and wage controls to "totalitarian" government. This idea of slippery slope from socialism to totalitarianism is less an argument than a naked hypothesis. Hayek offers no reason why one step down the path compels a nation to take a second or a third, let alone travel all the way into infamy. History suggests it does not. The persistence of "socialism" in postwar western European countries from roughly the 1940s to the 1980s is inconsistent with that story. So too are the paths of neoliberal regimes such as Pinochet's Chile, which have been characterized by brutalities no less than the former Communist regimes.

Hayek's argument also rests upon a sharp dichotomy between fixed and general laws, on the one hand, and elusively unstable measures such as wage and price controls, on the other. But it remains far from clear how to draw the line between law that enables and law that suppresses the spontaneous ordering of the market, or indeed whether such a line even exists. For example, are laws that require certain professions to be licensed market-enabling or contrary to the free market? Such restraints on entry were among the measures Hayek condemned. But what if certification solves an information problem for members of the public? That is, certification may be a means to screen for quality under conditions in which consumers are ill-equipped to do so—as in the case of doctors or lawyers. Absent such a screening mechanism, a market for certain services might collapse for want of trust.

There are other problems with Hayek's specific approach. For instance, it is not clear from his argument why wage and price controls cannot be fixed and stable. Nor is it obvious that legal interventions aimed at propping up a free market will always comply with Hayek's definition of the rule of law. Consider his later embrace of the judge-made common law. It is quite possible to imagine, say, a series of small and large changes to the common law of torts or contracts that are made through common-law decision-making with the aim of facilitating Hayek's spontaneous ordering. This might be, say, a shift from strict liability for some wrongs to a regime where the plaintiff must demonstrate a defendant was negligent in order to prevail. This sort of common lawmaking however, violates several of Hayek's criteria for the rule of law: it is not stable and cannot be known in advance, yet its purpose and effect might be market-enabling in the sense Hayek endorsed.

These worries go to how Hayek's theory of the rule of law works. They accept his understanding of freedom as defined solely in relation to the state. Of course, this definition has also long been contested. A long line of Marxian thinkers have focused on the appropriation of surplus labor by private actors as the main pressure on human liberty in industrialized societies. Building on comments by Karl Marx and V. I. Lenin, anticolonial writers charted the way in which Europe's free markets in Hayek's age depended on the violent exploitation of resource-rich colonies in Asia and Africa. And feminist thinkers analyzing women's historical experience have drawn out the pivotal role of private violence and rape as a key strut of various patriarchal, market-oriented systems. One does not need to reject the insight that the state can be a profoundly destabilizing agent of violence to see also that it has no monopoly on despotic force. But this recognition is hard to square with Hayek's vision of what counts as freedom.

Are there really that many versions of the rule of law?

We should ask whether these three branches of thinking about the rule of law are in fact all that different. Each reflects a commitment to liberalism of some sort. But if liberalism is understood as the project of somehow restraining the state, the variety of observed theories of the rule of law suggests that there are many ways of doing so. At the same time, it is also fair to say that the lawyer's "thin" rule of law has a foundational status. Both the political philosopher's and the economist's versions build on it, rather than displacing it. In both cases, such extension reflects a discontent with the moral thinness of the lawyer's rule of rule. Yet both of these "thick" versions of the rule of law then go on to propose quite ambitious, albeit divergent, moral and political projects for the legal system. It is fair to query, however, whether there is a legal system in existence that can sustain the weight of any such ambitious set of moral demands in their totality. The fact that we can articulate the possibility that law should do certain load-bearing work in the creation of a decent society does not in any sense mean that actual, existing legal systems are ever up to the job.

Chapter 5
Why does the rule of law survive?

A serious criticism of all contemporary theories of the rule of law is that they rely on magic. Each sets out the criteria that a legal system must meet in order to satisfy the rule of law. But none of them has much to say about how a legal system gets off the ground initially and achieves these criteria in a durable way. This is true for Albert Dicey, Lon Fuller, Tom Bingham, and Friedrich Hayek. Nor do they explain how the rule of law is sustained as a going concern. These are related but distinct concerns. Getting a decent legal system up and running is one thing. Keeping it in motion is another. At both points, there is a puzzle as to why powerful actors, in particular the ones wielding the levers of state violence, limit themselves within the bounds defined by law. Why should those who can dominate, that is, pause or desist when the law says no? Especially when a legal system is in its early days, this puzzle is likely to be especially pressing. If it is implausible to expect that Aristotle's "best man" will always rule—even Aristotle didn't think that—and if as a result people will in the end be thrown back at times on the protection of the laws without the safeguard of virtuous statesmen, how will be rule of law survive?

The puzzle is not a question of what, in theory or by definition, "law" involves. It is a crude question of realpolitik. It is no less important for that, however, and very far from academic—as recent Egyptian politics illustrates. In 2013 General Abdel-Fattah al-Sisi toppled an elected government in Egypt led by a political party called the Muslim Brotherhood. A decade later, there were tens of thousands of people—including many members of the former Brotherhood government—behind bars. The caseload of a shadowy body called the Supreme State Security Prosecution shot up from 529 cases in 2013 to 2,800 in 2021. When video of torture being used in a Cairo police station leaked in January 2022, the state prosecutor filed charges against the alleged victims for fabricating tales that undermined the state's authority. Intelligence services aligned with now-president al-Sisi, in any case, own several of the main television stations, so such allegations are never widely aired. And Egyptians abroad know that criticism can lead to their relatives at home being arrested. Egypt is very far from being a distinctive case. For many people around the world, across Asia, Africa, Europe, and the Americas, the most pressing question about the rule of law is not how it is defined. Rather, the pressing question is how it is set up and kept alive even in its most vestigial form. What continues to give the question bite is the fact that there is no universally accepted answer. Indeed, what is surprising is how little has been said on the matter that is persuasive.

Worries about the necessity, origins, and sustainability of the rule of law are hardly new. The French thinker Jean Bodin, the English philosopher Thomas Hobbes, and the American politician James Madison provide different vantage points on these concerns. In 1576, in *Six Books of the Republic*, Bodin proffered a definition of the sovereign as a supreme, indivisible, and enduring source of law for "subjects in general without their consent." No space remains for law as a constraint on this sovereign. The rule of law is thus superfluous. Hobbes is known now for his theory of how state power emerges in his famous 1651 treatise *Leviathan*. The sovereign that he describes in *Leviathan* is "not Subject to the Civil Laws." This is for the simple reason that it is the sovereign, the eponymous leviathan, who makes or repeals laws as it sees fit. As Hobbes puts it, "He that is bound to himself onely, is not bound." The sovereign is, by definition, created by an initial covenant, but is then unbounded by law. Hobbes thus does not share Dicey's belief that the fact that an English Parliament could act solely by enacting new law (and not, say, shouting orders at an army chief) is much of a constraint. Indeed, the very thought of setting "the Lawes above the Sovereign" struck Hobbes as an absurdity—an invitation to the sort of anarchy people had covenanted to avoid. If indeed there were another authority—say a court—that stood in earthly judgment over the initial sovereign's actions, this simply meant that this first entity no longer possessed the sovereign power. Such legalistic reform would simply replace the sovereign executive or parliament with the rule of lawyers. This, for Hobbes, was distinctly not an improvement.

Thinking about the project of a new American constitution at the end of the eighteenth century, Madison offered a variation on Hobbes's theme. On the one hand, he expressed skepticism about the value of "parchment barriers," such as bills of rights. (That he would later come around to penning one in 1791, in part out of political necessity, does not undermine his initial objection.) Instead, he suggested that the "real power" of the government lay in "the majority of the Community." However categorically a paper commitment was drawn, he worried, it could be blown adrift by the force of majority will. Dicey's cousin, the renowned jurist James Fitzgerald Stephen, would later capture a similar idea when he characterized parliamentary rule as "a mild and disguised form of compulsion." Minorities, Stephen thought, give way not because they are wrong but because they are simply weaker than majorities. If the law boils down to the latent threat of majority force, it should be noted, much of the rule of law's intrinsic appeal evaporates. Law is just the robber situation, writ large and with more bodies.

The problem of how the rule of law works is not entirely ignored by the leading texts. The English philosopher Joseph Raz, for example, was clear that legality arose only under quite specific social and political conditions. Yet this functional problem remains both a complex and a difficult one, arising in varying situations, for the rule of law can be pressured from several directions. The challenge in al-Sisi's Egypt springs from the security forces. In Hobbes's England, it came from a reckless monarch and civil disorder. In Madison's America, it was seen as bubbling up from a greedy, indebted rabble. It is not clear, though, that the same solution to the generic problem of rooting the rule of law is going to work in these three quite different practical and political contexts, given the different challenges in play. Despite this difficulty, the question of how the rule of law gets going and then persists is an important one. It is well worth understanding some of the leading responses that have been given over time, even if none end up being completely satisfactory. They are, after all, potentially the difference between the rule of law as something more than a theory and the hard realities of a torture cell in Cairo.

Building an institutional foundation for the rule of law

James Madison's answer to the "parchment barriers" problem looked back to Montesquieu's concept of the separation of powers. The French noble had suggested that the cure for an "atrocious despotism" lay in carving up government at the joint between three different branches—the executive, the legislative, and the judicial. But Montesquieu never clarified the precise relationship between this strategy of internal separation within government and the prevention of tyrannical outcomes. Madison tried to fill this gap.

Madison developed his theory while preparing for the Federal Convention of 1787 in Philadelphia, and then deepened it when defending the design of the 1787 Constitution. While framed as a matter of constitutional law, it can be extended to the context of law more generally without too much discomfort. In Madison's telling, the new national government would have three separate branches and national elections for both the presidency and Congress. Within this basic framework, Madison offered two concrete strategies for making the new legal system effective and durable without leaning on its leaders' virtue. The first turned on the motivations of those who were elevated to a national office. Madison thought that it was necessary for the individuals occupying those offices to identify themselves and their interests with their respective branches. He anticipated that they would thereby be motivated by a concern for their own branch to parry any overreach by another branch. The resulting crosscutting internal tensions within government would prevent any one branch from overreaching. In this way, "ambition" would "counteract ambition" and would elicit a government under law. Madison's second strategy turned on the possibility of splitting power between the national government and subnational units called states. This strategy has come to be known as a kind of "federalism." He hoped that the structure of federal elections would select for public-spirited politicians and that the state governments would serve as sentinels against the national government's abuse of centralized power. In this way, he offered a site-specific solution to the problem of rooting the rule of law. Federalism had no purchase, by contrast, in the context of Britain, a constitutional monarchy with Parliament at its core and minimal delegations of power, even now, to its outlying regions.

Madison's theory was at best a partial success. He conspicuously omitted any explanation for why officials would come to identify psychologically with their branch, as opposed to their political faction. Perhaps officials at times do come to have a belief that what matters is loyalty to their office. But it seems quite unlikely that the same level of identification with one's office will be evinced by politicians who are elected every two years, bureaucrats who remain in place for several years without facing an election, and judges who might haunt the bench for decades. Madison's theory of the rule of law's roots thus replaced the puzzle of why officials obey the law with the challenge of figuring out why and when officials come to identify with their offices.

He also never explained why the executive and legislature would be at loggerheads. They might instead decide to collude, potentially in ways that undermined, or even jettisoned, the rules of the game. This is also why it is no explanation of law's efficacy to say that officials depend on the laws that create their offices for their power in the first place. There is no particular reason why officials cannot or will not use the fact of their legal empowerment to modify or even eviscerate the formal limits on their legal powers. Without a steady hand at the tiller, therefore, it is quite unclear why the legal arrangement Madison anticipated would not capsize.

Madison's theory also relies on the existence of a federal structure in the United States. Not all nation-states have this feature. But it is not clear even in the American context why subnational bodies would be averse by default to the national government in the way that Madison describes. Why shouldn't a group of states collude with the national government to advance their aims at the expense of everyone else? Could that not elicit a distinct form of despotism? Indeed, the early American Republic's experience with the politics of slavery suggests that states could and did use the national government not just to shield themselves from the abolitionists' claims of justice, but also to advance their self-interested visions of international empire founded on the lash and the cotton gin.

It also does no good to observe that the Constitution that Madison designed remains in effect today—so it must have "worked." Even though the political arrangements of 1789 and 2024 share a common verbal form, it is quite clear that basic elements such as the presidency and the Supreme Court have changed beyond recognition. They have swelled in effectual power in dramatic and unanticipated ways, yielding institutions the Philadelphia delegates of 1787 could have barely imagined. In recent decades, moreover, legislative power has waned as Congress has become hamstrung by partisan polarization. At least from the perspective of a rule of law concerned with stability and predictability, therefore, it is just as plausible to say that Madison's plan, and his Constitution, foundered as it is to characterize it as a roaring success.

Finally, it is worth touching briefly on one institutional design solution that Madison did not advance: the creation of a judicial body that could discipline both the legislature and the executive. Powerful supreme courts have become increasingly common around the world, however, in the postwar period. The resulting pattern of "juristocracies" is controversial. Thinkers from the English philosopher Jeremy Bentham onward have expressed concern as to whether judges indeed will pursue the law in a neutral fashion, or in ways that advance their own generally elitist interests. The concern is particularly acute in constitutional regimes, such as the American one, in which the process of appointing judges is controlled by the national chief executive or a national legislature. Perhaps the best-known defense of the judicial role as a stabilizing, legalist force was offered by the early twentieth-century Austrian jurist and scholar Hans Kelsen. In the course of a sharp debate with conservative (later Nazi) jurist Carl Schmitt over the use of emergency powers in Weimar-era Germany, Kelsen offered a powerful argument in favor of courts as guardians of the basic law. Just as it cannot be assumed that legislators or chief executives will identify with their institutional homes, so too the question of whether judges promote or undermine the rule of law is an empirical one that must be assessed on a case-by-case basis. Such inquiry usefully begins by asking what kinds of institutions count as "courts" in the first instance: Do administrative tribunals of the sort Dicey disparaged, for example, count? With a definition in hand, it is possible to ask whether the involvement of a court will advance the rule of law—or why judicial action might create new costs or distortions.

It is therefore a mistake to identify the rule of law with any distinct set of abstract institutional choices. Such generalizations about the "best" institutional designs may not do large work in practice. Too much depends on how those bodies operate on the ground.

The rule of law and class conflict

A second way of thinking about the sources of the rule of law looks past the design of formal governmental institutions. It instead roots the rule of law in a wider context of social conflict. This approach draws on observations of Niccolò Machiavelli offered in the course of a longer historical discussion of the ancient Roman Republic. Machiavelli wanted to explain how it came to be that "liberty" could survive, and even thrive, under conditions of sharp social conflict. The core intuition that Machiavelli develops is simple, and transferrable to the rule of law. It is certainly possible to insist that the powerful crook their knees to the law. But they will do so only if they are forced to submit in this way by some countervailing force—and that force must be sought within society. It is most likely to take the form of the social classes normally at the receiving end of power's sword, and hence with the most to gain from a concrete realization of the abstract quality of legality.

Imagine a prince who wishes to maintain his power over a turbulent people, even as he must keep an eye on potential threats of foreign invasion or infiltration. No prince can do so alone. One possible strategy for the prince under these circumstances is to keep his population disorganized, fractured, dispirited, or otherwise unable to coordinate so as to threaten him. One problem with this approach, from the prince's vantage point, is that he may need to call the people to arms to repulse a foreign invasion. But a disorganized people will be hard to rally. Even a prince cannot defeat a foreign horde alone. He needs what Machiavelli calls *partigiani amici*, or "partisan friends." There are a few ways the prince garners such allies. A space at the political table is an option, as is a measure of fiscal redistribution. But with either of these tactics, the prince must be able to credibly commit to not reneging on his deal. If potential *amici* feared that the prince would take their aid and then spurn their political involvement or take back material benefits, they will not come to his aid in the first place. The rule of law—in the lawyer's thin sense of a general, predictable, and stable regime—is here a valuable good to potential allies. It enables the planning and construction of an orderly life by denying the prince the power to act in arbitrary ways. As such, it is both an intrinsically valuable good that the prince can supply in exchange for his *amici* to remain resolute in their support, and also a way of underwriting the prince's other bargaining chips. In addition, the rule of law has some side benefits for the prince. It might, for one, enable the emergence of a vibrant commercial sector. The virtues of a wealthy, taxable commercial society to an impoverished prince need little elaboration. And by publicly bending elites to the disciplinary rigor of common rules, it might further elicit a sense of shared fate. When it comes to foreign foes, it could act as the psychological cement that glues together the prince's sword.

A variation on this story hinges on a different worry of the prince—the need for fiscal credit with which to pursue state-building enterprises or else war. In an influential article about the English "Glorious Revolution" of 1688, the economist Douglass North and the political scientist Barry Weingast suggested that limitations on the previous largely unfettered powers of the Stuart monarchy arose out of the need for kings to be able to commit credibly to repay the Crown's debts and not to expropriate the property of its creditors. So long as those creditors are domestic, and not international, the rule of law might emerge as a device for credible commitment. Such commitment would hold so long as there were institutional structures that mediated the king's action and precluded arbitrary deprivations of property. At their inception, these devices might have greatest force for just one or two wealth creditor factions in society. Things might remain this way. Or the creation of these commitment devices might be the first step in a longer process, in which a range of other groups demand and obtain the rule of law's benefits by securing a place within the state's representative structures. Understood in these terms, the rule of law has an interesting vulnerability, which emerges only when there is a foreign bond market. For it is possible to imagine the rule of law unraveling as the credit-seeking sovereign turns to external actors such as foreign powers. A version of this intuition about a sovereign's need for credit has been formalized by contemporary political scientists, including Weingast. They use a branch of mathematics called game theory to model the social dynamics by which legality is produced. Their complex formal model implies that a decentralized pattern of private commitments to enforcing law can emerge when legal institutions display the positive traits of stability, openness, universality, and clarity. This is not quite the same as the rule of law, yet it offers an intriguing lens for thinking about how dispersed private action can generate something that looks like legal constraint of the state.

These accounts of the rule of law in one sense flip the Madisonian script. Rather than starting with the lawyer's question of how the state is structured, they begin with the sociologist's question of how different elements of society fit together. The more evenly balanced the different factions or classes are within a society, the more likely the rule of law is to emerge as a coordination mechanism. Conversely, with greater inequalities of wealth, and hence larger inequalities in access and capacity to use law, constraining force of the law is likely to founder. This suggests that societies characterized by yawning gulfs between the rich and the poor are not likely to develop or maintain the rule of law. While these sociological depictions of the rule of law support Hayek's argument about the virtues of predictability, they also undermine his assertion that the rule of law can tolerate—nay, even elicit—great inequalities of wealth.

Borrowing legitimacy

A final story about how the rule of law works again goes beyond formal institutions. It draws upon a regularity that can be observed most clearly in the early history of legal orders, but which likely persists in contemporary societies characterized by the rule of law.

Many early states borrowed the substantive content of their laws from a preexisting source, such as a body of religious law. Judaic, Islamic, and Vedic codes, for example, were all borrowed and grafted into states' laws. For example, the Dharmashastras of Vedic tradition, including Manu's 5,000-plus-line catalog of rules for daily life, emerged from scholarly Brahminic communities. They were absorbed into the law of early Indian empires. Under the Umayyad Caliphate of the seventh century CE, religious judges, or *qadis*, looked to Quranic texts to settle disputes. They also piggybacked on social norms local to conquered territories. Alternatively, law could be pinched from an illustrious ancestor. The Persian emperor Cyrus the Great cribbed his code from Mesopotamian predecessors. The first European codes, which in time would evolve into what is now called the civil law, drew in part on customary processes and in part on pieces of Roman law preserved thanks to the Byzantine Emperor Justinian's codification.

The early history of law is rife with plagiarism because budding states and empires had a dearth of coercive tools. Rather than simply creating their own laws, however, their leaders borrowed an established and respected body of existing religious or social norms. These already commanded respect and reverence from the people. By demonstratively aligning themselves with this law, by enforcing these prohibitions, and by abiding by their strictures, emperors and kings could gain public trust and credibility. But this strategy meant that they had to, in fact, follow and apply the borrowed rules. In effect, their actions were constrained by law insofar as that was necessary to maintain credibility.

The result, importantly, is not the full-throated rule of law. It is a leash patterned on whatever the borrowed rules happen to permit or forbid. These rules may be inclusive and enabling. Or they may be harsh and discriminatory. This pathway, in other words, is an uncertain causeway toward the rule of law. Yet it may also explain why the rule of law persists in modern societies. When a legal system emerges in harmony with widely shared moral and social values, it draws popular support from this fact. If popular support for a legal system and the governments that rest upon it depend on this harmony, those governments cannot violate popular moral and social codes with abandon without throwing their own legitimacy into question. They are in this way constrained by the very forces that nurture popular support for the legal system as a whole in the first place.

Why does the rule of law work (if it does)?

It seems eccentric to ask why the rule of law works. It manifestly does work in many of the circumstances in which it matters most. But, of course, this is true only from a certain point of view. For one thing, most people comply with law most of the time not because it is "law" but because it seems the correct, or natural, thing to do anyway. Murder is uncommon not really because it is illegal. It is rare because it strikes most of us as morally wrong. Law (including the law that binds officials) just looks stable, predictable, and effective because it largely tracks prelegal and extralegal religious or ethical codes that most of us, most of the time, find compelling on their own grounds. If law just compels us to do what we would anyway do, the observation of traits associated with the rule of law, such as integrity and persistence, should not be a surprise.

Further, it may be that we have become desensitized to the way in which the rule of law does fail in practice. Law simply does not, in fact, reliably constraint the powerful when it comes to their treatment of the weak. Even in countries with long and storied traditions of legality, there are communities that do not benefit from the stability and predictability of law. In the United States, for example, young Black men reasonably fear the police because of the staggering, and asymmetrical, rate at which they are killed in police encounters. Undocumented migrants are separated cruelly from their children; all are detained in filthy, dangerous cells. And violent conspiracies to murder the vice president and derail an election are met by many with a shrug of indifference. The blasé assertion that "the rule of law works" comes off a little tin-eared in these circumstances.

All the mechanics that have been discussed here largely take people as rational, selfish, even a little myopic—as social scientists conventionally do. They ignore, perhaps too quickly, the real possibility that officials and the public alike might come to value and identify with a rule-of-law project. They discount what Aristotle viewed as vital—the virtuous temperament to take law seriously. Yet moral aspirations of the sort that Aristotle would have recognized plainly do sometimes shape people's and officials' actions. The individual commitments of lawyers, judges, and officials to the rule of law have palpable effects in many consolidated legal systems. We should avoid the cheap cynic's view that just because it marks out a difficult aspiration, the rule of law cannot shape our world. Even if we cannot depend on the virtuous citizen's commitment to legality, we should gladly recognize it when it comes into being.

Chapter 6

Cultivating the rule of law in new lands

At the beginning of the twentieth century, the rule of law spoke in an Anglo-American lilt. Of course, Aristotle and Montesquieu were not British. But they were part of a widely shared intellectual heritage from antiquity and the Enlightenment claimed by Anglophone thinkers as somehow their own. Locke, Dicey, and Hayek all initially wrote for, and mainly influenced, an English-speaking audience. As described by Dicey and Hayek, the rule of law was understood as a quality that adhered in a single, territorially bounded state. It was thus largely a domestic matter. Not only the United Kingdom, but also many European countries and the United States, had greater or lesser far-flung territorial possessions. To the east, the Austro-Hungarian and Ottoman empires also subsumed nations into their own imperial frameworks. The rule of law did not extend evenly across these colonial empires. The Murderous Outrages Act of 1867 was not the only extraordinary measure enacted to accommodate the exigencies (or brutalities) of colonial rule. In February 1925 the eminent Indian jurist V. J. Patel could stand up in the Legislative Assembly of India and rattle off a half-dozen extraordinary statutory regimes that allowed colonial repression and the violation of basic rights. The era of European colonialism might therefore be characterized as a first era of "rule of law" globalization. It could also be characterized, however, as an era of persistent contestation over the quality of law, and the equality of its application as between rulers and the many-hued ruled.

After World War II, there was a new diffusion of the rule of law internationally. In July 1944 44 nations. met in Bretton Woods, New Hampshire, to agree upon a new international monetary framework centered on the US dollar. Out of Bretton Woods came the International Monetary Fund and the World Bank, institutions that were designed to help manage global currency politics and foster economic development. Fifty-odd years later, the World Bank's president would announce that the rule of law stood at the heart of economic progress. Development projects by the bank and other donor nations after that speech invariably included a "rule of law" component. Both the World Bank and private organizations have constructed measures of the rule of law, which are now used to rate countries. At the same time, the idea of the rule of law has come to be invoked by governments to advance very different understandings of the relationship of the individual to the state. Singapore and China, in particular, have imbued the rule of law with new meanings and new implications. They have articulated novel definitions of the rule of law nested within authoritarian political strategies. From a tool for facilitating the autonomous individual citizen, the rule of law has thus evolved into an instrument for maintaining centralized political control in the absence of democratic debate or choice. To disregard these developments as derogations or betrayals of the rule of law would be a mistake. It is better to comprehend them as evidence of how unexpectedly fertile the terminology of legality can be, albeit with arguably dismaying results.

In the postwar era, the phrase "rule of law" (or its synonyms in translation from the English) has been used in especially noteworthy ways by three influential actors: the World Bank, the Singaporean government led by Prime Minister Lee Kuan Yew, and successive generations of Chinese Communist Party (CCP) leadership. These adaptions repay attention because they involve self-conscious efforts to articulate alternative versions of the rule of law in conscious conversation with the Anglo-American tradition. In the cases of Singapore and China, a novel redescription of the rule of law has been tightly integrated into a dominant political party's efforts to monopolize political power. The result is a situation in which zones of legality and unbridled state power uneasily rub up alongside each other. In the more extreme case—China—the result can be what the brilliant German jurist Ernst Fraenkel called a "dual state," in which a functionally lawless "prerogative" state coexists uneasily with a more legalistic apparatus and perpetually risks collapsing into lawlessness. These histories illustrate concretely alternative evolutionary possibilities for the rule of law as an idea and as a lived political reality.

The World Bank's rule of law

There are many ways in which the rule of law has extended across national borders. The international human rights regime set in motion by the Universal Declaration of Human Rights in 1948 is one vector by which a variant of the rule of law has been internationalized. Another is the notion that international law more generally constitutes a rule of law between sovereign states. The most consequential and controversial "internationalization" of the rule of law, however, has unrolled along a different path. It takes Hayek's argument about the relation of legality to the free market as a starting point. This intuition, however, has been transformed in the process of being globalized. Hayek's core focus on freedom has been lost. Moreover, the resulting international rule of law is implemented using a set of tools that the Austrian did not anticipate.

In the last decades of the twentieth century, international economic institutions led by the World Bank took up the mantle of the rule of law. In a 2004 report, the bank contended that the rule of law helps a debtor government achieve a wide slate of goals. These include maintaining public order, promoting private sector growth, and fighting poverty. Given these connections, bank officials contended, development aid should be focused on two main ambitions. The first is establishing a market economy with property rights, minimal crime, and assured enforcement of contracts. The second centers on democracy and human rights. On the bank's view, these two goals are complementary. Without the rule of law, the bank's general counsel Ko-Yung Tung explained in 2002, neither "human dignity" nor "private sector growth" were possible. The connection drawn between legality and economic growth obviously echoed Hayek's formulation of the rule of law. But the bank drew more directly on studies in the 1990s suggesting that a nation's "legal origins"—and especially its links to the English common law—determined economic growth and foreign investment.

In practice, the World Bank's subsequent investments focused on the rewriting of economic regulation. This often meant reducing regulatory burdens on businesses and enlarging private markets. It also included other elements. In the mid-1990s, for example, the bank began pressing debtor nations to reform their judicial selection rules. The bank favored merit selection, a clear and strong judicial ethics code, and financial autonomy for the courts. This emphasis on the rule of law as a design principle for legal institutions also led to the emergence of a cottage industry of private and public indexes for measuring its quality. The bank itself, the Heritage Foundation, Freedom House, and the World Justice Project all developed different "rule of law indexes," emphasizing distinct combinations of institutional quality, property rights, and political freedoms.

There are two grounds on which development aid focused on the rule of law has been criticized. The first is that its institutional efforts often didn't take root in a durable way. In a flagship project in Venezuela in the late 1990s, for example, the bank spent roughly $52 million on physical infrastructure for the legal system, $18 million on courtroom administration, and $14 million on judicial training and administration. But it spent this money at the same time the populist government of Hugo Chávez was politicizing the courts. Whatever the bank's spending did was largely undone by Chávez's efforts at institutional capture of the judiciary. This suggests that the reform of legal institutions will fail absent a supportive political environment.

The second, perhaps more interesting, criticism is that the World Bank deploys the phrase "rule of law" largely as an instrument to advance a contestable set of deregulatory and market-enlarging policy goals. Critics complain that the bank treats law in practice merely as an instrument for "facilitating the private sector and the free market." This policy agenda, commonly called neoliberalism or the Washington Consensus, is condemned on its merits. It is blamed for driving up inequality and absolute levels of poverty. When foisted on a debtor nation as a condition for receiving much-needed financial assistance, it is also denounced as undemocratic. Consistent with this line of criticism, the economists who advance the "legal origins" theory, unlike Hayek, are quite explicit in evaluating the rule of law from the perspective of external, foreign investors. One leading voice in this debate, the Harvard economist Robert Barro, speaks of the rule of law in terms of "the attractiveness of countries as places of investment" in relation to contract enforcement, corruption, and the risk of appropriation. Read generously, Barro's animating assumption may be that the interests of external investors align with those of citizens because of a shared interest in growing a country's gross national product. Even this logic is, to say the least, controversial. It ignores profound disagreements about how new wealth should be distributed, whether and when inequality is tolerable, and the moral value of democratic self-rule.

The rule-of-law lens for development policy did not survive these criticisms unscathed. By the 2010s, the World Bank had shifted its analytic lens. A 2017 report, for instance, highlighted the idea of "governance," and suggested that the rule of law could only emerge over "a very long time" through "home-grown" processes. Whether or not the substance of World Bank interventions shifted, its strategy no longer focuses explicitly upon the rule of law as such. As a catalyst for economic development, the phrase appears to have somewhat lost its rhetorical luster.

Singapore's rule of law

In 1962 the prime minister of the city-state of Singapore, Lee Kuan Yew, gave a speech to the National University of Singapore's Law Students Society. He proclaimed that the rule of law was a vital foundation for the nation and its institutions. In a range of international forums and speeches since then, Lee and other Singaporean leaders have insisted that the city-state is characterized by both "the rule of law" and a well-paid and well-educated "independent judiciary." The legal system, they contend, is both consistent and reliable. It applies laws that are clear, consistent, general, prospective, public, and followed in practice by officials. The city-state's constitution further guarantees many of the individual rights of speech and association often associated with thicker versions of the rule of law. Lest there be any doubt about the matter, in 2007 Lee pointed to his own training in law at Cambridge University and the Middle Temple, one of London's inns of court, as evidence that he "knew the rule of law would give Singapore an advantage" upon independence.

A measure of this enterprise's success is the fact that Singapore was rated 17th in the World Justice Project's Rule of Law Index in 2023. The city-state stood a short way behind the United Kingdom, Japan, and Australia—but nine places above the United States. Singapore, in short, seems a paradigm of the rule of law under more than one definition of that term. The centrality of legality in its political culture has indeed been a major selling point for its leaders when they are touting the city-state's comparative global advantage to global firms. It would therefore seem a good example of a successful transnational grafting of the rule of law.

Yet things are more complicated. Since independence, Lee's People's Action Party has won all but a handful of seats in every legislature. Democratic opposition has been stifled. The government parries criticism with libel judgments or simply does not allow it to appear in print. Judges who step out of line in political cases lose expected promotions. And even when there are constraints of law placed upon the government's security powers, these have no meaningful effect. Singapore has all the trappings of the rule of law, in other words, but without all the benefits anticipated in respect to political life. If the government behaves in predictable and stable ways, allowing Singapore's economy to thrive, it is not because of law as such. It is because predictability in certain domains is of value to the reigning authorities.

This pattern of "a rule of law with a somewhat unconstrained state" can be illustrated with two incidents drawn from different moments in the city-state's history. In August 1966, a year after Singapore gained its independence, the new national assembly enacted a criminal law allowing corporal punishment for vandalism. The Vandalism Act was initially used mainly as a weapon against the left-wing opposition party Barisan Sosialis (Socialist Front). In response to bans on peaceful protest, left-wing activists had resorted to anti-US and pro-Vietcong graffiti tags. Defending the use of corporal punishment against these opposition operatives, Lee criticized magistrates and prosecutors who resisted the imposition of heavy punishments. Lee insisted that such resistance was motivated by a flawed belief that the "administration of justice" boils down to just "application of the law." Officials who declined to apply the Vandalism Act later found themselves out of a job. In Lee's view, they too had failed to grasp society's "fundamental" need to protect itself. The "law" upon which the rule of law rested was, in his view, properly understood as simply an instrument for the party that controlled the state to extend this control over society at large.

Almost 30 years later, the Vandalism Act again became a hot-button issue when an American-citizen teenager was convicted under the law. Responding to foreign criticism of its harsh penalties, Lee again insisted on the law's role in forestalling "chaos" and preventing the city-state going "downhill." He made this argument alongside an insistence that Singapore stood for a distinct set of "Asian values" in contrast to the weak, ineffectual, and disorderly West. The rule of law, for Lee and other Singaporean leaders, is a foundation for a distinct and different method of firmly ordering society through exemplary punitive violence. It is offered consciously as an alternative to a decadent West's weak-willed and wavering approach to order maintenance.

A second incident concerns the use of detention for national security ends. In 1988 four dissidents were arrested and detained without trial for allegedly plotting to undermine the government. Their lawyer asked the Singapore Court of Appeals to release them because the government had not followed procedures set forth in the Internal Security Act. The court agreed. It even offered the suggestion that later courts could intervene whenever the government used illegal or irrational tactics. The government complied with the release order, driving the men from the Whitely Road jail. And then, once they were outside the prison gates, it promptly rearrested them. Then it restarted the detention process under the precise terms of the statute. The government further amended both the constitution and statutes to clarify that courts did not have an important role in cases when state force was illegally or irrationally used. All this, by law and through law—and all to vindicate once again the state's iron fist.

Starting with Prime Minister Lee, Singapore's leaders have used both legislation and their own reputation for legality to undermine the capacity of legal institutions to limit powerful state actors. They have done so, however, while remaining within strictly legalistic bounds. In this endeavor, they have carved out a novel and distinctive understanding of the rule of law linked to their recitation of "Asian values." With this vision in hand, these leaders have not hesitated to laud this vision to Singapore's neighbors and competitors. They have, in effect, insisted that it is possible to comply with much of the lawyer's rule of law without binding the government's hands in any meaningful way. In the case of the Vandalism Act, this was done through pressure on magistrates and prosecutors. That this backstage influence flowed through informal and somewhat obscure back channels made it no less effective. In the case of the national security law, the government used its overwhelming numerical dominance of the legislative process for the same purpose. Such effective strategic manipulation of legal norms suggests that Dicey missed the mark when he described parliamentary supremacy and the rule of law as mutually entangled by definition. Where parliament is dominated by a single political movement committed to muzzling opposition, the legislature can mold the rule of law in ways Dicey had perhaps not anticipated.

Is this, then, the rule of law? One possible response is that Singapore illustrates something called "rule *by* law" when it comes to political matters. This phrase describes a state that uses law as an instrument of discipline and control, without in any way allowing it to constrain those wielding state power. In Singapore the rule by law is most clearly seen when threats to the People's Action Party's hegemony hove into view. Yet the Singaporean case also suggests that the line between a limiting rule of law and an enabling rule by law can be elusive. It is the same judges and prosecutors, after all, who enforced the Vandalism Act and the ordinary criminal law. A legal system can have elements of both "rule of law" and "rule by law." Indeed, the same people can be engaged in both projects simultaneously in different corners of their docket. Singapore also powerfully illustrates how a state can use law in subtly modulated ways in different domains. Like a suave Hitchcockian villain, it can commit credibly to investors and multinational firms that they will have a stable business environment on the one hand, while wielding the law as a knife against its political foes on the other.

The result is that expectations of legalistic constraint for political opposition are dramatically weaker than legality for everyone else.

"Governing China in accordance with law"

Around the time that the World Bank was becoming interested in the rule of law, that phrase also started to appear in Mandarin-language statements of Chinese Communist Party (CCP) doctrine. Its meaning, and the role that it has played in Chinese politics, has shifted since then. In its first few decades after the death of Chairman Mao in 1976, the CCP first liberalized the nation's economy and loosened controls on political speech, but then lurched back toward a more centralized and repressive economic and political model. Through these shifts, the rule of law "with Chinese characteristics" has remained an axiom of the party's doctrine.

The 1980s and 1990s were a period of rebuilding legal institutions in the wake of the Cultural Revolution. It was only in 1996 that President Jiang Zemin described an effort to "rule the nation in accordance with law" ("*yifa zhiguo*") while also building a "socialist country under law." Three years later, Jiang's language was added to the 1982 Constitution. And two years after that, China joined the World Trade Organization. This seemed to mark a shift toward the understanding of the rule of law pushed by global financial institutions. Indeed, the premier who followed Jiang, Hu Jintao, characterized China's legal system in terms that echoed the World Bank's understanding of the rule of law—emphasizing property rights, markets, and reliable credit provision. In 2007 the party's principal policymaking organ, the Politburo, described property rights as "part of the basic plan for implementing the law." In 2009 the Politburo met again to discuss "administration by law" and the "spirit of a socialist country under the rule of law." It seems that China was on a path of deepening its market economy while at the same time entangling its ruling elites in legal constraints.

But things did not work out that way. With the accession of Xi Jinping as both president and general secretary of the CCP in 2012, the place of *yifa zhiguo* in formal party doctrine seemed to ebb. There was a new focus on the primacy of Communist Party control. In a 2013 speech, Xi described the rule of law as subordinate to "the program of party leadership." Legal institutions were integrated into this project. The party had "groups" in most courts. Judges worked closely with both the Ministry of Justice and local governments. They took part, as a result, in local political campaigns on anti-corruption, birth control, respect for the elderly, and street cleaning. Under Xi, legal reforms also gave judges "lifetime responsibility" for their cases. Their dockets increased. But except for politically charged matters, the judges were pushed to behave in more professional, legalistic ways, and so decide nonpolitical cases according to the formal law. At times, and in some places, law reigned. But in a pinch it was subordinate to the project of party control.

Party doctrine also made clear that *yifa zhiguo* was to be understood as quite distinct from any "bourgeois" concept of law. On the understanding that came to dominate under Xi, law is not a constraint on the party. It is instead a mechanism through which the party overcomes the challenges of ruling a vast and varied nation, and of disciplining its fickle, easily tempted cadres on the ground. Law is a way of "rectifying individuals," not institutions. Under Xi, the rule of law is associated with the rule of virtue in anti-corruption campaigns. In 2018 he underscored the need to ensure that the state (but not the party) operate "strictly within the scope of the constitution and the law." His anti-corruption campaign not only tackled real graft. It also consolidated centralized control within the party. Legality became a double-edged knife. It disciplines the party's cadres in the state apparatus, but also empowers the central party. Indeed, when the National People's Congress Standing Committee added new national-security powers to Hong Kong's Basic Law in June 2020, and then used them to crush the city's pro-democracy movement and independent media, it could do so within the frame of legality.

As in Singapore's case, the rule of law in China is difficult to comprehend unless placed in its broader political context. Like Singapore, China is characterized by a one-party monopoly on effectual political power. The CCP's hold, however, is tighter and more closely hitched to a project of national greatness. Unlike Singapore, the party's dominance is reflected in the law's explicit terms. Article I of the 1982 Constitution defines party leadership as the "defining" characteristic of the polity. This constitutional text, however, is less important than the de facto authority of the party to act without regard to law. It is state institutions that are amenable to law; the party is subject only to its own rules. The Jiang and Hu periods were moments of relative party fragmentation. In the Xi era, the party has evinced fewer fault lines. It has extended its organizational reach into the private sector. New digital surveillance tools extend its control over individuals in both public and private spheres. At the same time, it has homed in upon a nationalist ideology that resonates with the Chinese public even as it has narrowed room for dissenting views. *Yifa zhiguo* is explicitly subordinate to this vision.

This evolution of *yifa zhiguo* can be understood in light of Machiavelli's insights into the social mechanisms through which the rule of law is produced. In his *Discourses*, Machiavelli posited that law might emerge as a constraint on the powerful under conditions of social conflict. The greater the threat of disruption from the plebeians, he thought, the more likely nobles would cede authority by coming under law. The ebb and flow of legality in China supports his point, with the CCP (and Xi) taking up the ermine of the prince. When the party's effectual power ebbed, as in the 1990s, a more complex understanding of the rule of law emerged. But as its power over society surged, the law became more of an instrument to advance the party's interests without any sense of reciprocal constraint upon the party-state.

Machiavelli also offers another illuminating point about why a prince would use the law. He observed that a prince would often find it valuable to delegate the thankless task of resolving disputes among subjects. Settling those disagreements often kindles enmity, he explained, without creating new allies. A similar logic helps explain why Xi's government has given the judiciary unprecedented responsibilities after a decade of stagnating reform. Doing so responds to genuine popular demands for dispute resolution at minimal political risk to the party.

This rule of law "with Chinese characteristics" is distinct from European and American analogs. Some observers have gone so far as to claim that it is not the rule of law at all, but a species of the "rule of man." Or it can be described as a "dual state," in which a zone of morally loaded ideas about legality coexists uneasily aside a domain of unbridled "prerogative" power. The border between these two zones, of course, is constantly at risk of collapsing, invariably to the detriment of legality.

Hybridizing the rule of law

When the rule of law migrates from the pastures in which it was originally cultivated, it metamorphoses dramatically. In the hands of Bretton Woods institutions, it became an instrument of macroeconomic discipline hitched to a neoliberal agenda. In a Singapore ruled by an austere barrister-turned-autocrat, it became a token of "Asian values" and the commitment to communal order over law. And in the (only notionally Communist) China of the twenty-first century, it has become *yifa zhiguo*, an instrument for reliably stabilizing centralized party rule.

But again, it is worth asking: Are all these varietals properly called the rule of law? There is no canonical account of the rule of law even in its home terrain. The understandings that have emerged in the multinational, Singaporean, and Chinese contexts cast light on the wide variety of aspirations to which the law can bend. And it is hardly clear that the older versions of the rule of law uniformly lack the "neoliberal" or authoritarian tincture that these examples have. Those prosecuted under the colonial Murderous Outrages Act, as applied in British India, might think not. Rather than being dismissed, *yifa zhiguo* is worth considering as a potentially durable model for the integration of law with concentrated political power. Given China's potential for growing geopolitical influence, not to say dominance, it is not implausible that *yifa zhiguo* will soon take on larger global importance. It may well be our future too. Or perhaps these case studies should not be embraced for the light they cast on the various ends a legal system can advance—but also for illuminating the perennial question, framed so eloquently by Lon Fuller, as to whether the law, standing on its own, has an intrinsic moral coloring worthy of our reverence.

Chapter 7
The rule of law condemned: Critics and crises

Sometimes, the rule of law is its own worst enemy. In Singapore, Prime Minister Lee Kwan Yew and his successors used the city-state's reputation for legality as an argument to deflect criticism of its authoritarian and antidemocratic policies. Legality for business made it easier to use arbitrary police powers against Lee's political foes. In contemporary Russia, public corruption allows considerable wealth to be drained from the state and major sectors of the economy. The oligarchs who benefit support the despotic and intolerant Putin government. This would be impossible if those oligarchs could not bank in an overseas destination with strong rule-of-law protections for property. The rule of law in London (such as it is) thus saps the rule of law in Moscow.

So, is the rule of law always a virtue? If the rule of law in one domain can undermine it in another, should it be assumed that legality is always both stable and benign? From the opening decades of the twentieth century, particular definitions of the rule of law have been contested. Dicey's rule of law not only neglected the oft brutal realities of British colonial rule. It also attracted the scorn of other leading British legal scholars, such as Ivor Jennings, for its blinkered dismissal of continental law and its perceived hostility to the welfare state. Lon Fuller's claims about the "internal morality" of law attracted a pointed demurrer from the British scholar Herbert Hart. And Hayek's connection of the rule of law to economic freedom and property rights has met repeated objections from left-liberal scholars. But these criticisms were focused. They did not reject categorically the idea of holding legal systems to an aspirational standard. They did not discard the hope that law could yield a beneficial kind of discipline.

Alongside these narrowly framed objections, though, other critics have launched categorical broadsides against the rule of law. They have challenged its stability and its desirability, not its details. The attacks travel on different ideological vectors. From the political left, the intellectual tradition seeded by Karl Marx generated scathing condemnations of the ideological, even delusional, quality of what it labeled "bourgeois legalism." The most enduring was penned by a Soviet jurist, Evgeny Pashukanis, who saw law as inexorably shaped by the commodification logic of industrial capitalism. A different, equally potent attack came from the political right. The rule of law, it posited, is a feeble and incoherent makeweight. It ignores core, existential realities of political life—namely the sovereign's brute act of decision and the pervasiveness of mortal conflict. It thereby deludes its advocates into a complaisant ignorance about the incoherent and self-defeating quality of the rule of law as a foundation for liberal self-rule. The most incisive and influential version of this argument came from a controversial German jurist, Carl Schmitt.

The criticisms of Pashukanis and Schmitt presaged three of the most pressing crises experienced by the rule of law almost a century later. First, the rule of law is under pressure from economic inequalities flowing from the present configuration of capitalism. Second, the twenty-first century has been characterized by a series of shocks from outside the ordinary flow of politics, as well as the responsive deployments of emergency powers that threaten the rule of law. These crises include terrorism and viral pandemics such as SARS, MERS, and COVID-19. In response to these shocks, governments around the world reached for emergency powers to detain, control movement, intrude on privacy, and stifle speech. In some cases, these powers introduction has also accelerated existing patterns of rule-of-law decay. Third, and not unrelatedly, economic and cultural dislocation have seeded a series of "populist" political movements. These follow Schmitt in understanding politics as a deadly contest between the nation and its enemies. Leaders carried to power by such movements often show a blatant disregard for legality. In the acute cases of Hungary and Venezuela, they have turned legal institutions against the democratic process and their own people.

That Pashukanis and Schmitt anticipate in their writings some of the thorny issues raised by contemporary crises is not coincidental. Both men wrote their key works in the 1920s. This also was a decade of turmoil. Revolutionary fervor, political violence, and civil strife across central and eastern Europe placed the viability of legalism in serious doubt. Both men's lives, indeed, intersected with regimes of violent atrocity—Nazism and Stalinism—albeit in quite different ways. These contact points between their work and the abject failure of legalism (and, more importantly, humanity) complicate any reading of their work today. Proximity to evil also brought ruin to both. But it also seems to have charged their work with a particular kind of insight.

Pashukanis

Born in 1891 in what is now Lithuania, Evgeny Pashukanis became a Bolshevik in 1912. He rose through the ranks of the new USSR, becoming one of its leading jurists and a vice-commissioner for justice. His magnum opus of the 1920s, *The General Theory of Law and Marxism*, was reprinted several times. It was also quickly translated into German and Italian. By the 1950s, jurists on the other side of the Iron Curtain, including Lon Fuller and Herbert Hart, singled out this work as "ingenuous" and "important" even as they resisted its foundational premises. Pashukanis's theory of law, of course, was anchored in Karl Marx's economic theory and his historical materialist analysis of history.

The first centered labor as the source of economic value. The second identified changes to the technological forms of economic production as motors of historical progress toward first a capitalist and then a communist state. One implication of Marx's position was the centrality of society's economic structure (the base) and the derivative quality of its political and legal forms (the superstructure). This base-superstructure distinction points toward a highly limited role for law as merely a reflection of, and perhaps a means to reproduce, capitalists' dominance of the working classes. On this view, the values associated with the rule of law—stability, consistency, publicity, and the like—should be decried, not celebrated. If the law boils down to the interests of the capitalist class, then it deserves no respect, and the rule of law should be abandoned even as an aspiration.

Pashukanis's distinctive contribution was a more subtle depiction of law. Drawing on early passages of Marx's *Capital*, he identified a "deep connection" between the distinctive forms adopted by law and the "commodity form." For Marx, a commodity is not just a good or service. Rather, it is a "mysterious" device through which value-creating labor is transformed into a universally recognized form that is especially amenable to market exchange. On Pashukanis's telling, any society that is even remotely based on the "exchange of commodity values" will necessarily adopt the familiar forms of law. The only form of law, that is, is "bourgeois law." So, when the dynamic of historical materialism leads to the dissolution of capitalism, this will also lead to the "disappearance of the juridical factor" from social life.

Law, in this view, arises from the conflict between specific private interests. So not every kind of social organization involves law. Pashukanis pointed to military regulations and train timetables as forms of rule-based organization that are not "law," because they do not arise out of class conflict. At the same time as he stressed conflict, Pashukanis insisted that law is not simply a reflection of the triumphant "class interests" of the bourgeoisie or, more generally, the "prevailing relations" between the classes. Instead, law embodies and creates an order of abstract relationships through which the creation and ensuing flow of commodities in a market economy can be arranged. A legal relation is one that has been abstracted from the context in which production occurs. The law decants the material results of actual "dominance and subservience" into a set of formally equal relations suitably planed down to enable the smooth flow of market transacting. This commodity-based economic system needs what only the law can supply: "a person endowed with rights on the basis of which he actively makes claims." That is, a basic function of law is the fashioning of a formally equal right-bearing subject, which is an obvious fiction, in order to meet the demands of commodity exchange through the market. The organization of law around this rights-bearing subject assumes a distinction between private interests and the public's interests. Property can be exchanged with the conscious "will" of the owner, even as the linkage between labor and the commodity unfolds unseen "behind people's backs." Having obscured from view the actual springs of value, law then offers its subjects what Pashukanis describes with biting irony as a "rare thing"—the noble lie that all those interacting in the market are "absolutely free and equal" to act based on their own free will. The commodity form of law will be overcome, however, in the transition Pashukanis anticipates from capitalism to communism.

Pashukanis's view of law and its origins suggests that the very features that the rule of law celebrates—abstraction, generality, and even-handedness—are just tools enabling a commodity-based market economy. Here, Pashukanis's theory has a surprising kinship with Hayek's. Both underscore the relation of law to market ordering. But for Pashukanis, the law does not just enable markets, it hides "behind people's back" the facts of unjust extraction of surplus value. The problem with law, on this telling, is not that it simply reflects a capitalist class's interest. Rather, law is objectionable because the basic units through which it organizes society emerge from an undesirable logic of exploitation, commodification, and mystification—and indeed are crafted to enable and extend that logic. The link between law and injustice is beyond curing. It runs too deep for that.

Predictably, Pashukanis's theory shares some of the problematic qualities of Marx's. It is framed, most importantly, around a class-centered theory of historical materialism that attracts little support today. In an age in which the value of environmental and intangible assets is better recognized, a labor-centered theory of value also is of questionable value. Another puzzle concerns causation: How can law be an outcome of the commodity form when the legal relations of property are needed in the first place to organize exploitative production? Nevertheless, Pashukanis's text offers a distinctive way of thinking about the relationship between patterns of economic activity and ownership, on the one hand, and the law, on the other. It gestures to the possibility of root-and-branch criticism of the project of legality based on its relationship to economic processes. Subsequent thinkers have offered more narrow-gauged critiques. But Pashukanis's is striking in the sweep and depth of its indictment. His was neither the first nor the last such root-and-branch critique of law, but it remains one of the most interesting and sophisticated.

Fifty years later, it would be another Marxist who would offer the most forceful extension, and partial repudiation, of Pashukanis. The English Marxist historian Edward Thompson published a short book on an English statute called the Black Act of 1723. A creature of the corrupt government of Robert Walpole, the Black Act contained a gamut of new capital crimes. These targeted poachers in the royal forests and were largely enforced through summary proceedings. Thompson explains how the act was a rather crude instrument of the ruling class. It enclosed common resources for the benefit of the wealthy. But, he cautions, those brought to book under the act still felt a sense of "legal wrong." The communities under the act lived near royal forests and depended upon them for nourishing game. For the law to work effectively on these communities, Thompson explained, it was not enough for it to mirror class relations. It had to have its own freestanding logic, traits, and evolution. In particular, it had to appeal to what Thompson called "standards of universality and equity." Echoing Pashukanis, Thompson here stressed law's claim to abstraction and universality.

At the same time, however, Thompson broke from Pashukanis. On Thompson's view, it was not enough for the law to be "evidently partial and unjust." If this were so, it would "mask nothing, legitimate nothing." The law instead, occasionally, actually be just. It must also bind the Walpoles of the world, who could not simply shrug off the rules that bind everyone else, "or the whole game would be thrown away." The result was something different from the raw exercise of arbitrary power sometimes called "rule by law." Even when it is just a "nuisance" for the ruling classes, Thompson concluded, the rule of law "is an unqualified human good."

This remark occasioned a good deal of consternation among scholars on the left. Perhaps few of them were directly acquainted, however, with the fear that pervades a society ruled by law without anything like the rule of law. Few have experienced what Montesquieu called despotism. And so few can credit the partial, perhaps very small, gain celebrated by Thompson as a major achievement without being overwhelmed by the injustices that remain. The same cannot be said for Pashukanis. In the late 1920s he became the object of increasing criticism by Stalinists for his claim that law is necessarily bourgeois. This was an obvious embarrassment for a regime that championed a strong state, channeling repression through the legal forms of the secret police and the show trial. He was called a "wrecker" and a "Trotskyite saboteur." Long after the slaughter of the kulaks and the Holodomor, a desperate Pashukanis published a series of groveling paeans to Stalinism. It did not work. In 1937 he was liquidated—one more body on the heap for "socialist legalism."

Schmitt

During the Weimar period in Germany, Carl Schmitt was a young yet renowned law professor, first in Bonn and then in Berlin. In this period, he published a series of books about the legal and political convulsions of the young republic. Among the most important were *Political Theology* (1922), *The Crisis of Constitutional Democracy* (1923), *The Concept of the Political* (1927), and *Constitutional Theory* (1928). These works are still the bedrock of his contemporary reputation. They offer a carefully qualified defense of democratic rule, albeit on terms that many now find unappetizing. They also sketch a novel pattern of dichotomies to organize legal and political thought. Schmitt's sharp distinctions—between the rule and the exception, the friend and the enemy, the commissarial and the sovereign dictator, among others—define and bound his signature contribution. But the way they hang together remains sharply debated. Their reading now is complicated by what happened next in his career: on May 1, 1933, Schmitt joined the ascendant Nazi Party. For three years, he sat atop the legal profession, penning justifications of Hitler's extermination of political foes ("The Führer protects the law") and the Nuremberg race laws ("The Constitution of Freedom"). He was ousted in 1936—like Pashukanis, for his apparently insufficient loyalty to the regime. This period in Schmitt's career nevertheless creates a difficult and divisive question: To what extent should his earlier works be read as anticipating and even advancing toward the embrace of fascist rule organized on principles of racial purity and violent suppression of democratic opposition? Even if it is assumed that Schmitt was an opponent of National Socialism before 1933 (as some evidence suggests), should his arguments be situated in the movement toward Nazi rule? Or would such a gloss simply embody prejudicial hindsight?

However these questions are answered, Schmitt's critique of the rule of law has plainly been influential. It prefigures some of the worries brought to the fore by the populist explosion and serial emergencies of the early twenty-first century. At its core, his theory holds that the system of autonomous rules that make up a legal system is something of an illusion. The ambition typically thought central to the rule of law—of constraining the power of a governing class under stable, predictable, and transparent rules—is an illusion. Law for Schmitt depends on sovereign authority, and sovereign authority inevitably proceeds though action and not the written word. It is the unmediated, raw fact of a sovereign's decision, unbounded by law, upon which social order ultimately rests. Behind Schmitt's sovereign lies a vision of politics defined not by bargaining between groups, or even the latent conflicts Pashukanis posited. Politics, taught Schmitt, is a matter of active, mortal, and violent conflict against an enemy. Only a homogeneous people, capable of recognizing its enemy through the decisive action of a sovereign, can be a nation.

The seed of Schmitt's case against the rule of law is found in his stark assertion that "[s]overeign is he who decides on the exception." Law is often imagined as a system of general rules. But these can never accommodate effectively all unexpected emergencies. It is simply inevitable, contended Schmitt, that unanticipated crises will strike. At that point, there must be a decision about whether there is indeed an emergency, and, if so, what should be done. This power, moreover, is logically unbounded. It is inconsistent with—it negates—the force of otherwise generally applicable written law. This is because a legal order can exist in the first place only if there is a decision by the sovereign that *no* emergency obtains. Hence law as a system persists only at the sufferance of the sovereign. Any sovereign decision on the exception, moreover, must come as if from nothing, unbounded by law or morality. And if that power of decision does not exist, what follows is worse: the "status of states" is simply lost. Schmitt also rejected all efforts by the liberal constitutional state to cabin the exception. On his telling, this is simply logically impossible. It is the exception alone that "confirms not only the rule but also its existence." A legal order, in consequence, can only exist if there is a sovereign decision; accordingly, the liberal ideal of an autonomous body of law that guides and constrains the state's actions is an illusion.

The model of sovereignty that Schmitt offers is linked to his distinctive understanding of the "political." For Schmitt, the creation of a modern state requires action by an "organized people." The people become a state when they coalesce into a singular form that "decides for itself the friend-enemy distinction." In this way, the sovereign is prior to law. It comes into being by electing an existential foe. In an odd parallel to Schmitt's contemporary George Orwell, this theory of law rests on the claim that our core political identity is a matter of who we target for our "Two Minute Hates." For Orwell, of course, that prospect was profoundly dystopian. In contrast, Schmitt thought that the weak and confused liberal state "evades and ignores" the political, and instead finds refuge from the basic decisions of politics in the desultory purgatory of "ethics and economics."

There is a whiff of mysticism in Schmitt's aphorisms. When he talks of the exception as "real life" breaking through the "crust of a mechanism that has become torpid by repetition," he comes close to sounding like a New Age guru leading a workplace retreat. A persuasive reading of Schmitt's work thus needs to begin by situating it in the wider context of German *Existenzphilosophie*. This was a current of thinking, exemplified by Oswald Spengler's *Decline of the West*, that diagnosed a catastrophic moral crisis afflicting all European values at the dawn of the twentieth century. In consequence, it proposed that only the brute fact of human existence had any significance or value.

Many will also resist Schmitt's claims about the sovereign's decisions defining the law, along with his related view that emergencies cannot be regulated in advance. Citing Dicey, they will point to the availability of after-the-fact legislative scrutiny and the indemnification of justified lawbreaking. Schmitt's insistence on the exception appeals not so much to reasoned argument, they will say, but to the arrant braggadocio of the bully. Nor will all be persuaded that politics must be organized around an "existential" friend-enemy distinction. For many of us, that sounds like a depiction of how politics goes wrong, not a description of its core.

Nevertheless, Schmitt's work has an abiding appeal because it points toward the difficulty of managing catastrophic shocks. It forces attention to the problem of law's undertow of brute force. Further, Schmitt's analysis of the exception points toward an important weak spot in most versions of the rule of law. This is the possibility that legalism's enemies gain political power and use that power to dismantle the legal constraints on their authority. Schmitt says that this possibility can never be avoided, since no system of written legal rules can ever be entirely constraining. As he puts it in *Constitutional Theory*, a legislature "is in no conceivable manner bound by its statutes." Rule-of-law theorists, in other words, go awry when they forget that the legal system necessarily rests on a political constitution, and that there is always a risk of rupture between that political agreement (in "real life") and the laws on the books. Even if one finds the language of sovereignty opaque or obsolete, this is surely an important observation, one that resonates even if it not an analytic truth.

Like Pashukanis's commodity theory of law, Schmitt's aphorisms on the exception are pitched at a very high level of abstraction. For both theorists, there is a question of whether their general claims about "legal form" and the necessary limits of government by statute bear fruit today. Indeed they do. In the early twenty-first century, even the lawyer's thin rule of law has come under strain in the territories it has historically called home. Three lines of stress flow from the diagnoses of Pashukanis and Schmitt—inequality, populism, and emergency. These are not the only lines of strain that might be mapped. It is true that starting with different definitions of the rule of law might lead to a focus on quite different crises. Those influenced by Dicey's hostility to administrative courts might finger the growing power of national bureaucrats. Or they might bemoan the migration of lawmaking authority from national legislatures to supranational bodies such as the European Union and the infamous "troika" that emerged in the European debt crisis. Or they might raise a worry about the growing power of high courts around the world to set national policy—say, on Brexit or morals legislation—without any real guiding law. But a choice is necessary. And like any choice between specifications of the rule of law, a selective canvassing of its present crises necessarily reflects a judgment about what values the law is best understood to further.

Economic and other inequalities

In April 2016, the chief executive officer of Facebook, Mark Zuckerberg, vowed to the US Senate that he was "not opposed to regulation," so long as it was the "right regulation." Less than five years later, Facebook would shut down its news feed as a way of putting pressure on the Australian government to forego new laws aimed at social media platforms. That government relented. In the United States, a series of disclosures about social media's troubling effects, including by Facebook whistleblowers, did not lead to new American legislation. Perhaps not coincidentally, in the same year that it shut down its Australian news feed, Facebook spent more than $5 million on lobbyists in Washington, DC. The company's market dominance (in Australia) and the wealth it flexed (in America) in effect purchased a shield against law.

But nothing Facebook did violated the law. Neither in Australia nor in the United States did its actions undermine the guidance role law plays. Yet it still seems plausible to say that the rule of law is troubled by the company's actions. So, at some point do background wealth inequalities run afoul of the rule of law? Theorists of the rule of law divide on this question. On the one hand,

Hayek concludes that such disparities cannot be avoided and that the state's redistributive efforts would necessarily be lawless. On the other hand, it might seem that generality, publicity, and the like are virtues only if they are coupled to effective access to justice for all. This means not just open courts. It also requires a population that has the material and psychological resources to access those courts readily in order to press their rights, rather than being preoccupied by where to find their next meal or rent payment.

The early twenty-first century is an opportunity to test these competing views. In Europe and the United States during the first decade of that century, wealth was concentrated to an extent not seen for a hundred years. In Europe, for example, the poorest half of the population owned less than 5 percent of all property, while the richest 10 percent had 55 percent of all property. In the United States, the divide was wider still. The poorest half of the people possessed barely 2 percent of property. Meanwhile, the wealthiest tenth claimed about 72 percent of those resources. Can the rule of law thrive, or even be sustained, under such conditions?

There is evidence that wealth disparities do translate into serious failures in the rule of law. A first concern is illustrated by the Facebook example. If the wealthy can gerrymander the reach of laws, the rule of law may continue to play a guidance function, but its guidance is partial. Its instructions will anticipate and accommodate the desires of the wealthy, while biting hard on the projects of the impoverished. A law that is guided by the wealthy, but that guides only the poor, is an odd and partial realization of the rule of law. Such a legal system is also amenable to the political philosopher's objection that it no longer secures justice for all, or at least on terms that could be justified to all. It is further vulnerable to the economist's objection that regulators (including legislators) can be captured by cartels and monopolists. Parliaments and regulatory agencies might then be persuaded to craft the law to allow firms to externalize costs or extract monopoly rents. This imposes social harms. It also undermines the free market the law is supposed to sustain. As the examples of Lee's Singapore and Xi's China might be taken to suggest, the rule of law seems to be creating the conditions for its own decay.

Economic and political power can also influence the way that existing law is enforced. This can undermine even the rule of law's modest guidance function. In 2020 the US trial judge Jed Rakoff observed that even as his New York–based court was sentencing thousands of poor people to prison every year, corporate executives were effectively immune from prosecution for white-collar crimes with "only the rarest of exceptions." The practical and political difficulties of bringing such cases, he explained, kept prosecutors' focus on the less wealthy. When a criminal prosecution is brought, moreover, the effects of economic inequality often shape how the law is applied. The result is a gap between the "law on the books" and a "law on the ground" that varies in heft depending on a person's wealth. This effect is most pronounced when the criminal justice system is "adversarial," as in the United States and the United Kingdom. An adversarial system depends on the litigants, not the court, to gather and sift evidence. Hence the quality of litigation outcomes turns on the relative resources each side has. When there is a large gulf between the wealthy and the poor, the state will also find it cheaper, and easier, to pursue and coerce the less-well-off. Most modern legal systems are hard to navigate without expert assistance. In practice, wealth inequalities degrade procedural and substantive rights closely linked to the rule of law. Formal protections against physical abuse or miscarriages of justice, for example, can be rendered moot if the poor have no practical way to assert them. Although the state can remedy some of these problems with legal aid, in both the United States and the United Kingdom this is stingily doled out.

Economic disparities are not the only kind of inequalities that can sap the rule of law. Imagine a society scarred by patriarchal beliefs (or perhaps just look around). Women are likely to find it more difficult to invoke the law. The case of the 22-year-old Iranian woman of Kurdish extraction, Mahsa Amini, is instructive. Amini was arrested, tortured, and killed by Tehran's so-called morality police in September 2022. Her death provoked furious protests, many led by women ordinarily marginalized in public life. One protester explained why Amini's death triggered such anger in terms Locke or Montesquieu would have recognized: "You don't know what they will do to you." Could a more crystalline rendering of the rule of law (or, more accurately, its absence) be offered? A society characterized by profound gulfs in social power—whether economic, gendered, racial, or religious—is a society at pervasive risk of arbitrary, despotic harms.

There is, then, cause to doubt Hayek's conclusion that economic disparities are compatible with the rule of law. The rule of law does not demand anything more than rough equality. But it is rocked by gross, if not by minor, inequalities. But just as the medieval church's practice of selling indulgences deservedly attracted the mockery of Chaucer and the wrath of Luther, so too the sight of the wealthy spending their way out of regulation, and out of punishment, makes a mockery of contemporary law's moral aspirations. The problem is one that both Pashukanis and Schmitt would have appreciated, even if they did not pin it down: the fruit of the very market system enabled by the rule of law can derail the possibility of an orderly, generally applied set of laws.

The era of emergencies

In one sense, Schmitt was correct: the early twenty-first century has been an era of public emergencies. From the terrorist attacks on New York and Washington to the macroeconomic spasm of 2008–2009 to the global COVID-19 pandemic of 2020, governments have repeatedly been confronted by new and immediate threats to public welfare for which they had not fully planned. Perhaps these crises should have been anticipated. But they were not. Instead, governments responded on the fly. Often, they drew on so-called emergency powers. On Schmitt's view, this should have been fatal to the rule of law. What followed, however, has been more complex.

Emergencies come in many registers. National security, macroeconomic, environmental, and public health crises all vary in scale and consequence. Sometimes the emergency and the state's response focus on small groups or minorities. Post-9/11 security policy focused on Muslim and Arab minorities in the West, for example. Others implicate whole populaces as vectors of harm. The COVID-19 pandemic is an illustration of this. Some, again like COVID-19, are global in scale. Others, like Hurricane Katrina, which hit the American state of Louisiana in 2005, or the flooding in Pakistan's Sindh Province in 2022, are localized. Some happen quickly. Others, like climate change, unfold so slowly that human beings appear incapable of processing what their own eyes reveal. Emergencies demand different sorts of knowledge and varying responses. It is often said, rather casually, that security emergencies draw on expertise and information that only the state possesses. In contrast, the critical knowledge in a public-health emergency will often be dispersed, and in private hands. Contra Schmitt, there is no one kind of emergency—and likely no one kind of desirable state response.

Emergency powers, indeed, vary dramatically in practice. An archetype is the ancient Roman Republic's practice. Its Senate would instruct the two consuls to appoint a "dictator" for up to six months. The dictator would then deal with the threat to the republic without keeping an eye on the law. And then he would step down. Contemporary legal regimes vary in locating emergency authorities either in a constitution or in statutes enacted by legislatures. Laws can also be temporary or permanent, although temporary measures often outlive their formal sunsets. Where a constitution provides for strong judicial review, courts may also play a role defining the outer perimeter of emergency powers.

The rule-of-law criticism of emergency powers has several strands. A first worry is that emergency rule violates elementary demands of the lawyer's rule of law. Under the Roman model, for example, the dictator acted without legal guidance. A contemporary emergency law or constitutional provision might be interpreted so broadly that the actions that follow are effectively arbitrary and potentially despotic. A second, related concern is that emergency powers will be used to unravel the larger legal order from within. The dictator simply does not leave office. Egypt's military ousted an elected government in 2013, for example. By the time it organized elections in 2018, the sole contender running against former general Abdel Fattah al-Sisi supported the military's continuing rule. Not surprisingly, al-Sisi retained power. This is a concrete example of how the "exception," as Schmitt termed it, might negate the general rule.

Third, an emergency can involve derogations of basic rights understood to be part of a thicker conception of the rule of law. A legal system that embraces indefinite detention and torture, Lords Bingham and Steyn insist, cannot claim the rule of law's mantle. After the 9/11 attacks, legal scholars in the United States rushed to propose legal devices to enable indefinite detention and torture—safe in the knowledge that it would be young Muslim men, not them, who suffered. Lawyers for the government offered ingenious yet disingenuous arguments to enable those practices despite statutory bans. They showed that the derogation of basic rights with raw violence can be dignified with a thin patina of statutory license. This is more evidence of how law can decay from within. Exceptional violence can also undermine the possibility of law playing a guidance role in daily life without statutory change. Egyptians under al-Sisi experience the ordinary police as lawless despots despite formal bans on torture.

Fourth, measures adopted during an emergency can leak into "ordinary" times, thereby undermining rule-of-law-adjacent rights. In the United Kingdom, Parliament responded to the 9/11 attacks in the United States with the Anti-terrorism Crime and

Security Act 2001, the Prevention of Terrorism Act 2005, and the Terrorism Act 2006. All these measures, which enhanced the government's powers of coercion and detention, remain on the books. Two decades after the first prisoners were brought to the US naval base at Guantánamo Bay, more than 30 remained imprisoned there a under a statutory regime that allows unlimited detention following the barest, most deferential of court review. Indeed, the judicial review that has been exercised made no palpable difference to the pattern of detentions.

The American and British responses to 9/11 thus illustrate some of the risks that emergencies present to the rule of law. In contrast, the global response to the COVID-19 pandemic shows how legal systems can adapt Montesquieu's idea of the separation of powers to mitigate legality-related damage. Around the globe, pandemic responses often unfolded under newly minted statutes, with either judicial or legislative supervision, and often through negotiation with regional and city governments. In the United Kingdom Parliament enacted a measure specific to the pandemic allowing additional powers for 21-day periods. France and Liberia created special committees of lawmakers to oversee pandemic responses. Where the executive acted before a law could be passed, legislatures reviewed those actions. In Taiwan the legislature reviewed and gave after-the-fact authorization to border controls imposed by the president in early 2020. Courts also intervened both to stymie lawless government action and to force the state to protect its citizens. In Romania and El Salvador judges curbed lockdown and detention powers. Pakistan's high court, in contrast, urged the government to enact new legislation after having invalidated an executive decree shutting down businesses. Measures to counteract a global pandemic that kills more than six million people in the span of two years cannot be counted a "success" under any ordinary use of the English language. Nevertheless, the global pattern of national responses to COVID-19 disarms, rather than supports, Schmitt's claims about the unraveling force of the exception.

Not all pandemic responses conformed to rule-of-law ideas. Turkey's government used a flurry of presidential and ministerial circulars, press announcements, and ad hoc decision-making in its response. Lacking any statutory framework, this reaction was unpredictable and arbitrary. Perhaps the most serious derogations of rule-of-law values arose when governments used the pandemic to advance a preexisting agenda antithetical to legality. The May 2020 Hungarian law giving Viktor Orbán "extraordinary and unlimited" decree powers is the leading example. Another is the Chinese state's exploitation of the pandemic to arrest leading figures of the democracy movement in Hong Kong, such as the 81-year-old lawyer Martin Lee. Such exceptional uses of exceptional powers do not suggest that emergency powers cannot ever be squared with the rule of law. Rather, they gesture at a risk to legality that is implicit within certain styles of emergency responses as much as in ordinary governing.

Populism and law's end

From Latin America to central Europe, the first decades of the twenty-first century have been characterized by electoral wins by political leaders and parties often called "populist." A leading definition of that term takes populism to be a political strategy based on a "moralistic imagination of politics" organized around the confrontation between a morally purified "people" and a corrupt "elite." This is a variation on Schmitt's friend-enemy distinction. It can be discerned in Hugo Chávez's comprehensive assault on Venezuelan democracy, Boris Johnson's suspension of Parliament in pursuit of Brexit, and Donald Trump's various efforts to instrumentalize American diplomacy and criminal justice for personal or political benefit.

Hungary provides the best example, however, of how a thick rule of law can be transformed into a legal regime imposing no meaningful constraint on the arbitrary use of state power. Upon gaining control of the parliament in 2011, Orbán's Fidesz party issued a proclamation that Hungary had regained the "right and power of self-determination." This identified the party with the nation. By implication, it ranked the political opposition as disloyal, even alien. Invoking a mythic ideal of the nation, Fidesz used its parliamentary supermajority to push through a raft of constitutional amendments. The number and lines of electoral districts were redrawn to the party's advantage. A new "Media Authority," appointed by Orbán, was invested with broad powers to supervise and sanction broadcast, print, and online media. A parliamentary Data Protection Commissioner was abolished. Hungary's courts, previously a bastion of liberal and legalist values, were dismantled and reconstructed. The chief justice was prematurely dismissed. A change to the mandatory retirement age forced more than 100 judges to leave office early. The scope of constitutional review was changed. It became harder for citizens to bring legal challenges. It became easier for the government to seek the court's exercise of jurisdiction. Among the 319 statutes enacted in the first 18 months of Fidesz's rule were completely new civil and penal codes. In effect, the party used a host of seemingly proper changes to law as a means of disabling almost every mechanism whereby its power could be checked. The net result is more akin to China's *yifa zhiguo* than to the rule of law described by Dicey, Hayek, or Bingham. It would have been recognizable to Schmitt, as an exemplar of the sovereign dictator enacting the politics of enmity, and to Pashukanis, who would have insisted that law's constraint on power had always been illusory—and that all that remains, in Budapest, as elsewhere, is the commodity form.

Yet the rule-of-law ideal has also been mobilized against democratic decay in Hungary: the European Parliament and Council issued a communication affirming it as "one of the founding values of the European Union." The parliament and council defined the rule of law as a condition in which "all public powers always act within the constraints set out by law, in accordance with the values of democracy and fundamental rights, and under the control of independent and impartial courts." To give force to these concerns in respect to Hungary, the European Union has deployed a "conditionality mechanism" for fiscal transfers. Hence a post-COVID recovery disbursement of 5.6 billion Euros was delayed. In September 2022 the European Commission suggested that it would withhold an estimated 7.5 billion euros from Hungary based on corruption and rule-of-law concerns. It remains to be seen whether these supranational efforts at rule-of-law promotion are more successful than the World Bank's efforts of the late 1990s and early 2000s. Should these measures prove ineffective—say, because Hungary is able to muster enough political support within the EU to head them off—the result may be greater internal differentiation across European countries in terms of legality.

What remains of law

A dictator of Brazil in the 1930s, Getúlio Vargas, is reputed to have said, "For my friends everything, for my enemies the law." So, indeed, it has often been. Tycoons, emergencies, and populists can sap the rule of law. Sometimes, legality itself can prove a remarkably effective instrument for unraveling its own best aspirations. This happens not only via spillovers, from London to Moscow say, but also when the forms of law are deployed for the purpose of creating a state in which one party or faction exercises close, even total, control. A disposition of reverence toward the law is usually a boon to legality. It becomes a liability when regimes exploit the all-too-human habituation toward obedience and respect for the law with a contempt for their subjects. Law then is cleaved and fractured into something that fosters fear and despotism, not any recognizable form of liberty, equality, or security.

Epilogue

What then will become of the rule of law? The gathering pace of crises—the collapse of middle classes in Europe and the Americas, emergencies in the shadow of climate change, and the accumulating strength of populists and other autocracies—bodes ill for the near term. There is, however, a deeper, more subtle reason for doubt.

Law is a technology. It allows the state to govern without an exhausting surfeit of arbitrary violence. The rule of law captures an aspiration toward the tolerable use of this tool. This book has aimed to flesh out the plausible range of such aspirations, and also show how those hopes can sour. But any technology can be superseded if a cheaper alternative emerges. Since the 1990s, there have been important advances in the material science and mathematics of computing. These have allowed larger pools of data to be collected and analyzed to new ends. Using a set of techniques called "machine learning," it is possible to exploit data so as to predict information that is not in the original training data set. The result is a fine-grained technique for discerning hidden personal information, predicting behavior, and shaping preferences without the subject's knowledge. This predictive insight can be marshaled to control and direct human behavior without the need for general, abstract laws.

Among states, the global leader in the use of these tools is China. Its party state has extended a thick network of public surveillance cameras equipped with facial recognition tools, a so-called social credit system for tracking "trustworthy" behavior, app-based movement tracking justified by the pandemic but extended beyond it, and a comprehensive screening and control of social media and Internet activity. These technological tools complement the use of arbitrary arrests and "re-education camps" all too familiar from earlier despotisms. Yet the innovations by the Chinese party-state have allowed it to map and control individual behavior without recourse to law. The formal, written legal system, as a result, is becoming less important for guiding individuals' behavior. Of course, China still uses law in many ways. Law thus remains a tool for ensuring internal party discipline and extending control geographically. Yet the further new technological forms of prediction and control diffuse, the less important law will be. Even if law is never retired, it may fade in importance. The rule of law may become less important than the rule of machines.

What then? These new techniques of social control may have destabilizing effects on the basic building blocks of the rule of law elsewhere. Machine-learning tools could jettison pre-programmed decision rules, and instead infer decision rules from large pools of data. A written network of rules and judicial precedent would no longer be needed. Machine decisions would also no longer be scrutable to lawyers or lay persons. As a result, a new elite of programmers and data scientists would emerge to husband society in lieu of today's elite of lawyers. If this new elite ever develop their own moral aspirations for governing with the same civilizing potential as the rule of law, the ensuing norms would likely have a different flavor and varying content from the tradition formally inaugurated by Dicey.

The rule-of-law tradition mapped in this book can be said to have emerged at a specific time and place, albeit by drawing on intellectual resources that long predated that moment. One day, technological change could make it feasible to declare that tradition at a definitive and distinct end. By offering a very short summary of the aspirations impounded into the phrase "rule of law," this book has furnished some basis for readers to decide for themselves whether this imagined future would be a matter of celebration or despair.

References

Note that sources are listed in the order they are used in each chapter. Page numbers for important quotations are also included.

Chapter 1

Joseph Raz, *Practical Reason and Norms* (Oxford: Oxford University Press, 1975).

Lord Bingham, "The Rule of Law," *The Cambridge Law Journal* 66, no. 1 (2007): 67.

John K. M. Ohnesorge, "The Rule of Law," *Annual Review of Law and Social Science* 3 (2007): 99.

Ewan Smith, "The Conception of Legality under Xi Jinping," in *Law and the Party in China: Ideology and Organisation*, ed. R. Creemers and S. Trevaskes (Cambridge: Cambridge University Press, 2021).

Gabor Tóth, "Illiberal Rule of Law? Changing Features of Hungarian Constitutionalism," in *Constitutionalism and the Rule of Law: Bridging Idealism and Realism*, ed. M. Adams, A. Meuwese, and E. Ballin (Cambridge: Cambridge University Press, 2017).

Yuji Vincent Gonzales, "Duterte: Sometimes, Rule of Law Can Be Stupid Proposition," *Inquirer.Net*, November 14, 2016, https://newsinfo.inquirer.net/844177/duterte-sometimes-rule-of-law-can-be-stupid-proposition#ixzz7ggFNrTAx, for Duerte quote.

Howard Johnson and Christopher Giles, "Philippines Drug War: Do We Know How Many Have Died?," *BBC News*, November 12, 2019, https://www.bbc.com/news/world-asia-50236481.

John Finnis, "The Unconstitutionality of the U.K. Supreme Court's Prorogation Judgment," Policy Exchange, October 2019, https://policyexchange.org.uk/wp-content/uploads/2019/10/The-unconstitutionality-of-the-Supreme-Courts-prorogation-judgment.pdf.

Mark Elliott, "Constitutional Adjudication and Constitutional Politics in the United Kingdom: The Miller II Case in Legal and Political Context," *European Constitutional Law Review* 16, no. 4 (2020): 625.

Kevin Molloy and Colin Witcher, "The Rule of Law: An Analysis of the Supreme Court Decision in Miller/Cherry," Church Court Chambers, September 26, 2019, https://churchcourtchambers.co.uk/article/the-rule-of-law-an-analysis-of-the-supreme-court-decision-in-miller-cherry-by-kevin-molloy-and-colin-witcher/.

Johan Steyn, "Guantanamo Bay: The Legal Black Hole." *International and Comparative Law Quarterly* 53, no. 1 (2004): 1–15.

Shawn Walker, "Hungary Passes Law That Will Let Orbán Rule by Decree," *Guardian*, March 30, 2020, https://www.theguardian.com/world/2020/mar/23/hungary-to-consider-bill-that-would-allow-orban-to-rule-by-decree, for the "extraordinary and unlimited government powers" quote.

Benjamin Novak, "Hungary Moves to End Rule by Decree, but Orban's Powers May Stay," *New York Times*, June 16, 2020, https://www.nytimes.com/2020/06/16/world/europe/hungary-coronavirus-orban.html.

Polly Botsford, "Rule of Law: Hungarian Government's Emergency Covid-19 Legislation Draws Sharp Criticism," International Bar Association, May 11, 2020, https://www.ibanet.org/article/B9C2F848-0633-4963-B977-9E2FAB392967.

Fernanda Pirie, *The Rule of Laws: A 4,000-year Quest to Order the World* (Profile Books, 2021).

Jeremy Waldron, "The Concept and the Rule of Law," *Georgia Law Review* 43, no. 1 (2008): 1.

Jack Nicas and André Spigariol, "To Defend Democracy, Is Brazil's Top Court Going Too Far?," *New York Times*, September 26, 2022, https://www.nytimes.com/2022/09/26/world/americas/bolsonaro-brazil-supreme-court.html.

"Facebook Reverses Ban on News Pages in Australia," *BBC News*, February 23, 2021, https://www.bbc.com/news/world-australia-56165015.

Chapter 2

Charles S. Maier. *Leviathan 2.0: Inventing Modern Statehood* (Cambridge, MA: Harvard University Press, 2014).

Carne Lord, ed., *Aristotle's "Politics"* (Chicago: University of Chicago Press, 2013); for all quotes, see paragraphs 1279a to 1287a.

Steve Wexler and Andrew Irvine, "Aristotle on the Rule of Law," *Polis* 23, no. 1 (2006): 116.

Judith N. Shklar, "Political Theory and the Rule of Law," in *The Rule of Law: Ideal or Ideology*, ed. Allan Hutchinson and Patrick J. Monahan (Toronto: Carswell, 1987).

Brian Z. Tamanaha, *On the Rule of Law: History, Politics Theory* (Cambridge: Cambridge University Press, 2004).

John Phillip Reid, *Rule of Law: The Jurisprudence of Liberty in the Seventeenth and Eighteenth Centuries* (Dekalb: Northern Illinois University Press, 2004).

Niccolò Machiavelli, *The Discourses* (London: Penguin Books 1970).

Clare Jackson, *Devilland: England under Siege 1588–1688* (London: Penguin, 2021), for background on the early seventeenth century in England.

Thomas Hobbes, *Leviathan*, ed. Richard Tuck (Cambridge: Cambridge University Press, 1997, first published 1652).

John Dunn, *The Political Thought of John Locke* (Cambridge: Cambridge University Press, 1969).

Felix Waldmann, "John Locke as a Reader of Thomas Hobbes's *Leviathan* : A New Manuscript," *Journal of Modern History* 93, no. 2 (2021): 245.

John Locke, *Two Treatises of Government and a Letter Concerning Toleration*, ed., Ian Shapiro (New Haven, CT: Yale University Press, 2008), mainly chapter five of the second treatise, from where all the quotes are drawn.

Judith Shklar, *Montesquieu* (Oxford: Oxford University Press, 1987).

Montesquieu, *The Spirit of the Law*, ed. Anne M. Cohler et al. (Cambridge: Cambridge University Press, 1989); the quotes are from pages 3, 16–29, and 155–157.

Duncan v. Louisiana, 391 U.S. 145, 169 (1968) (Black, concurring), contains his views on the "origins of due process."

Nicolas Vincent, *Magna Carta: A Very Short Introduction* (Oxford: Oxford University Press, 2012).

Tamar Herzog, *A Short History of European Law* (Cambridge, MA: Harvard University Press, 2018).

Max Radin, "The Myth of Magna Carta," *Harvard Law Review* 60, no. 7 (1947): 1060.

Michael Forsythe, "Magna Carta Exhibition in China Is Abruptly Moved from University," *New York Times*, October 14, 2015, http://www.nytimes.com/2015/10/15/world/asia/china-britain-magna-carta-renmin-university.html?-r=.

Chapter 3

Charles S. Maier. *Leviathan 2.0: Inventing Modern Statehood* (Cambridge, MA: Harvard University Press, 2014), for the historical context of Dicey's career.

Mark Walters, *A. V. Dicey and the Common Law Constitutional Tradition: A Legal Turn of Mind* (Cambridge: Cambridge University Press, 2021).

Christian R. Burset, "Redefining the Rule of Law: An Eighteenth Century Case Study," *American Journal of Comparative Law* 70, no. 4 (2022): 657.

Mark D. Walters, "Dicey on Writing the Law of the Constitution," *Oxford Journal of Legal Studies* 32, no. 1 (2012): 21.

Martin Loughlin, "A. V. Dicey and the Making of Common Law Constitutionalism," *Oxford Journal of Legal Studies* 42, no. 1 (2022): 366.

A. V. Dicey, *Introduction to the Study of the Law of the Constitution* (Indianapolis: Liberty Fund, 1982); the quotations are from pages 110–118 and 268–273.

Elizabeth Kolsky, "The Colonial Rule of Law and the Legal Regime of Exception: Frontier 'Fanaticism' and State Violence in British India," *American Historical Review* 120, no. 4 (2015): 1218.

Dylan Lino, "Albert Venn Dicey and the Constitutional Theory of Empire," *Oxford Journal of Legal Studies* 36, no. 4 (2016): 751.

Albert Venn Dicey, *Lectures on the Relation between Law and Public Opinion in England during the Nineteenth Century* (London: Routledge, 2017); for the quotation, see pages 309–310.

W. Ivor Jennings, *The Law and the Constitution* (London: University of London Press, 1933).

Chapter 4

Bush v. Gore, 531 U.S. 98 (2000), 128–129, for Justice Stevens's quotation.

Liora Lazarus, "Brexit in the Supreme Court," *The Conversation*, September 26, 2019, https://theconversation.com/brexit-in-the-supreme-court-when-populists-attack-the-rule-of-law-everyone-loses-124302.

Judith N. Shklar, "Political Theory and the Rule of Law," in *The Rule of Law: Ideal or Ideology*, ed. Allan Hutchinson and Patrick J. Monahan (Toronto: Carswell, 1987), 1, for "ruling class chatter."

Raymond Geuss, *Not Thinking Like a Liberal* (Cambridge, MA: Harvard University Press, 2022).

John Gardner, *Law as a Leap of Faith: Essays on Law in General* (Oxford: Oxford University Press, 2012), especially pages 196–220.

Nicholas W. Barber, "Must Legalistic Conceptions of the Rule of Law Have a Social Dimension?" *Ratio Juris* 17, no. 4 (2004): 474.

Giuseppe Tomasi Di Lampedusa, *The Leopard* (New York: Everyman's Library, 1991), for the quote about change.

Joseph Raz, "The Politics of the Rule of Law," *Ratio Juris* 3, no. 3 (1990): 331.

Frederick Wilmot-Smith, *Equal Justice: Fair Legal Systems in an Unfair World* (Cambridge, MA: Harvard University Press, 2019).

Antonin Scalia, "The Rule of Law as a Law of Rules," *University of Chicago Law Review* 56 (1989): 1175.

Timothy Endicott, "The Impossibility of the Rule of Law," *Oxford Journal of Legal Studies* 19, no. 1 (1999): 1.

Meir Dan-Cohen, "Decision Rules and Conduct Rules: On Acoustic Separation in Criminal Law," *Harvard Law Review* 97, no. 3 (1984): 625.

Norman Yoffee, *Myths of the Archaic State: Evolution of the Earliest Cities, States, and Civilizations* (Cambridge: Cambridge University Press, 2005).

Konatsu Nishigai, "Two Types of Formalism of the Rule of Law," *Oxford Journal of Legal Studies* 42, no. 2 (2022): 495.

Andrew G. Walder, *Agents of Disorder: Inside China's Cultural Revolution* (Cambridge, MA: Harvard University Press, 2019).

Tom Bingham, *The Rule of Law* (London: Penguin, 2011).

Ronald Dworkin, *A Matter of Principle* (Cambridge, MA: Harvard University Press, 1985).

Tim Congdon, "When Margaret Read Friedrich," *Times Literary Supplement*, March 2, 2012, 23.

F. A. Hayek, *The Road to Serfdom* (Chicago: University of Chicago Press 1944), with quotations drawn from pages 57–63, 71–79, 94–95, 101, and 121.
F. A. Hayek, *The Constitution of Liberty* (London: Routledge, 2020), especially pages 180–203.
F. A. Hayek, *Law, Legislation, and Liberty 1: Rules and Order* (Chicago: University of Chicago Press, 1973).

Chapter 5

Robert Paxton, *The Anatomy of Fascism* (New York: Knopf, 2004).
"Too Many to Count," *The Economist*, July 23, 2022.
Jean Bodin, *On Sovereignty* (Cambridge: Cambridge University Press, 1992).
Thomas Hobbes, *Leviathan*, ed. Richard Tuck (Cambridge: Cambridge University Press, 1997, first published 1657), with quoted passages on pages 84 and 224.
James Fitzjames Stephen, *Liberty, Equality, Fraternity* (New York: Holt & Williams, 1873), with quotes from pages 27–28.
Jeremy Waldron, "Separation of Powers in Thought and Practice," *Boston College Law Review* 54 (2013): 433.
Isaac Kramnick, ed., *The Federalist Papers* (London: Penguin, 1987).
Matthew Karp, *This Vast Southern Empire: Slaveholders at the Helm of American Foreign Policy* (Cambridge, MA: Harvard University Press, 2016).
Niccolò Machiavelli, *The Discourses* (London: Penguin Books 1970).
Stephen Holmes, "Lineages of the Rule of Law," in *Democracy and the Rule of Law*, ed. Adam Przeworski and José María Maravall (Cambridge, Cambridge University Press: 2003), with quotations from pages 35–37.
Douglass C. North and Barry R. Weingast, "Constitutions and Commitment: The Evolution of Institutions Governing Public Choice in Seventeenth-Century England," *Journal of Economic History* 49, no. 4 (1989): 803.
Gillian K. Hadfield and Barry R. Weingast, "Microfoundations of the Rule of Law," *Annual Review of Political Science* 17, no. 1 (2014): 21.
Aziz Huq, "What We Ask of Law," *Yale Law Journal* 132 (2022): 326.
Mark Condos, "Licence to Kill: The Murderous Outrages Act and the Rule of Law in Colonial India, 1867–1925," *Modern Asian Studies* 50, no. 2 (2016): 479.

Chapter 6

World Bank, *Initiatives in Legal and Judicial Reform*, at 2 (Washington, DC: World Bank, 2004), http://www-wds.worldbank.org/external/default/WDSContentServer/WDSP/IB/2004/03/01/000012009_20040301142827/Rendered/PDF/250820040Edition.pdf.

Gordon Barron, "The World Bank and Rule of Law Reforms," Working Paper No 05-70, Development Studies Institute, 2005, 9.

Rafael La Porta, Florencio Lopez-de-Silanes, and Andrei Shleifer, "The Economic Consequences of Legal Origins," *Journal of Economic Literature* 46, no. 2 (2008): 285.

Kenneth W. Dam, *The Law-Growth Nexus: The Rule of Law and Economic Development* (Washington, DC: Brookings Institution Press, 2007).

Mila Versteeg and Tom Ginsburg, "Measuring the Rule of Law: A Comparison of Indicators," *Law & Social Inquiry*, 42, no. 1 (2017): 100.

Tor Krever, "Quantifying Law: Legal Indicator Projects and the Reproduction of Neoliberal Common Sense," *Third World Quarterly* 34, no.1 (2013): 131.

Robert J. Barro, "Democracy, Law and Order, and Economic Growth," in *2013 Index of Economic Freedom*, ed. Terry Miller, Kim R. Holmes, and Edwin J. Feulner (Washington, DC: Heritage Foundation, 2013), 41.

World Bank, *Governance and the Law* (Washington, DC: World Bank, 2017), https://www.worldbank.org/en/publication/wdr2017, especially page 14.

Sek Keong Chan, "The Courts and the 'Rule of Law' in Singapore," *Singapore Journal of Legal Studies* (2012): 209.

Gordon Silverstein, "Singapore: The Exception That Proves Rules Matter," in *Rule by Law: The Politics of Courts in Authoritarian Regimes*, ed. Tom Ginsburg and Tanir Moustafa (Cambridge: Cambridge University Press, 2008).

Jothie Rajah, "Punishing Bodies, Securing the Nation: How the Rule of Law Can Legitimate an Urban Authoritarian State," *Law and Social Inquiry* 36 (2011): 945.

Jothie Rajah, *Authoritarian Rule of Law: Legislation, Discourse and Legitimacy in Singapore* (Cambridge: Cambridge University Press 2012), with Lee's quotes about the rule of law reproduced on pages 30–31 and 38.

Ewan Smith, “The Rule of Law Doctrine of the Politburo,” *China Journal* 79, no. 1 (2018): 40; contains the quotations from Presidents Jiang, Hu, and Xi.

Kwai Hang Ng, “Is China a Rule-by-Law Regime?” *Buffalo Law Review* 67 (2019): 793.

Taisu Zhang and Tom Ginsburg, “China's Turn toward Law,” *Virginia Journal of International Law* 59 (2019): 306.

Qianfan Zhang, “The Communist Party Leadership and Rule of Law: A Tale of Two Reforms,” *Journal of Contemporary China* 30, no. 130 (2021): 578.

Ruiping Ye, “Shifting Meanings of Fazhi and China's Journey toward Socialist Rule of Law,” *International Journal of Constitutional Law* 19, no. 5 (2021): 1859.

Chapter 7

Ernst Fraenkel, *The Dual State: A Contribution to the Theory of Dictatorship* (Oxford: Oxford University Press, 2018).

Lon L. Fuller, “Pashukanis and Vyshinsky: A Study in the Development of Marxian Legal Theory, *Michigan Law Review* 47 (1948): 1157.

H. L. A. Hart, “Review of *The Communist Theory of Law*, by Hans Kelsen,” *Harvard Law Review* 69, no. 4 (1956): 772.

E. B. Pashukanis, *Law and Marxism: A General Theory* (London: Ink Links, 1978), with quotations from page 57–63, 81, 95–96, and 112–115.

E. P. Thompson, *Whigs and Hunters* (London: Penguin Books, 1975), especially pages 203–209.

Richard Wolin, “Carl Schmitt, Political Existentialism, and the Total State,” *Theory and Society* 19, no. 4 (1990): 389.

Carl Schmitt, *Political Theology: Four Chapters on the Concept of Sovereignty* (Chicago: University of Chicago Press, 2005), quotes on pages 11–15.

Carl Schmitt, *The Concept of the Political* (Chicago: University of Chicago 2007).

Carl Schmitt, *Constitutional Theory* (Durham, NC: Duke University Press, 2005).

Emily Birnbaum and Caitlin Oprysko, “Facebook Lobbying Surges to $5M amid Whistleblower Uproar,” *Politico*, October 21, 2021, https://www.politico.com/news/2021/10/21/facebook-lobbying-uproar-516443.

Thomas Piketty, *A Brief History of Equality* (Cambridge, MA: Belknap Press, 2022), for data on rising inequality.
Jed Rakoff, "Getting Away with Murder," *New York Review of Books*, December 3, 2020, https://www.nybooks.com/articles/2020/12/03/getting-away-murder-executive-prosecution/.
Vivian Yee and Farnaz Fassihi, "Women Take Center Stage in Antigovernment Protests Shaking Iran," *New York Times*, September 26, 2022, https://www.nytimes.com/2022/09/26/world/middleeast/women-iran-protests-hijab.html.
John Ferejohn and Pasquale Pasquino, "The Law of the Exception: A Typology of Emergency Powers," *International Journal of Constitutional Law* 2, no. 2 (2004): 210.
Tom Ginsburg and Mila Versteeg, "The Bound Executive: Emergency Powers during the Pandemic," *International Journal of Constitutional Law* 19, no. 5 (2021): 1498.
Joelle Grogan and Julinda Beqiraj, "The Rule of Law as the Perimeter of Legitimacy for COVID-19 Responses," in *Routledge Handbook of Law and the COVID-19 Pandemic* (London: Routledge, 2021), 201–213.
Jan-Werner Müller, *What Is Populism?* (Philadelphia: University of Pennsylvania Press, 2016).
European Commission, "Communication: Further Strengthening the Rule of Law within the Union—State of Play and Possible Next Steps," COM(2019)163 final (Brussels: European Commission, 2019); contains the quotes about the rule of law.

Further reading

There are a number of excellent recent academic books on the rule of law. Among recent studies, a few books and articles stand out. To begin with, Brian Z. Tamanaha's *On the Rule of Law: History, Politics Theory* (Cambridge: Cambridge University Press, 2004) is an excellent primer. Further, Paul Gowder's *The Rule of Law in the Real World* (Cambridge: Cambridge University, 2016) offers a novel theory of the rule of law, based around the idea of equality. A sequel, *The Rule of Law in the United States: An Unfinished Project of Black Liberation* (London: Hart Publishing/Bloomsbury, 2021), extends his argument. Another recent, profound meditation on the rule of law is Gerald Postema's *Law's Rule: The Nature, Value, and Viability of the Rule of Law* (Oxford: Oxford University Press, 2022). There are also excellent stand-alone chapters on the rule of law in Martin Loughlin's *Foundations of Public Law* (Oxford: Oxford University Press, 2010) and N. W. Barber's *The Principles of Constitutionalism* (Oxford: Oxford University Press, 2018).

Those searching for more focused philosophical discussions should look to Jeremy Waldron's and Martin Krygier's excellent and insightful articles. Both have written extensively on a wide variety of issues related to the rule of law. An example of the former is Waldron's "The Concept and the Rule of Law," *Georgia Law Review* 43, no. 1 (2008). (Waldron has also written an excellent entry on the rule of law for the online *Stanford Encyclopedia of Philosophy* that is very rewarding.) An example of Krygier's useful work is his article "Four Puzzles about the Rule of Law: Why, What, Where? And Who Cares?," *Nomos* 50, no. 1 (2011).

Finally, readers interested in the historical development of the law should consult the magisterial volume by Fernanda Pirie, *The Rule of Laws: A 4,000-Year Quest to Order the World* (New York: Profile Books, 2021), which covers, as its title suggests, the development of law and legal institutions over the sweep of recorded human history.

Index

For the benefit of digital users, indexed terms that span two pages (e.g., 52–53) may, on occasion, appear on only one of those pages.

A

B

C

D

E

S

T

U

V

W

Y

Z

ENVIRONMENTAL LAW

A Very Short Introduction

Elizabeth Fisher

Environmental law is the law concerned with environmental problems. It is a vast area of law that operates from the local to the global, involving a range of different legal and regulatory techniques. In theory, environmental protection is a no brainer. Few people would actively argue for pollution or environmental destruction. Ensuring a clean environment is ethically desirable, and also sensible from a purely self-interested perspective. Yet, in practice, environmental law is a messy and complex business fraught with conflict. Whilst environmental law is often characterized in overly simplistic terms, with a law being seen as be a simple solution to environmental problems, the reality is that creating and maintaining a body of laws to address and avoid problems is not easy, and involves legislators, courts, regulators and communities.

This Very Short Introduction provides an overview of the main features of environmental law, and discusses how environmental law deals with multiple interests, socio-political conflicts, and the limits of knowledge about the environment. Showing how interdependent societies across the world have developed robust and legitimate bodies of law to address environmental problems, Elizabeth Fisher discusses some of the major issues involved in environmental law's: nation statehood, power, the reframing role of law, the need to ensure real environmental improvements, and environmental justice. As Fisher explains, environmental law is, and will always be, inherently controversial.

www.oup.com/vsi

Human Rights

A Very Short Introduction

Andrew Clapham

An appeal to human rights in the face of injustice can be a heartfelt and morally justified demand for some, while for others it remains merely an empty slogan. Taking an international perspective and focusing on highly topical issues such as torture, arbitrary detention, privacy, health and discrimination, this *Very Short Introduction* will help readers to understand for themselves the controversies and complexities behind this vitally relevant issue. Looking at the philosophical justification for rights, the historical origins of human rights and how they are formed in law, Andrew Clapham explains what our human rights actually are, what they might be, and where the human rights movement is heading.

www.oup.com/vsi

LAW
A Very Short Introduction
Raymond Wacks

Law underlies our society - it protects our rights, imposes duties on each of us, and establishes a framework for the conduct of almost every social, political, and economic activity. The punishment of crime, compensation of the injured, and the enforcement of contracts are merely some of the tasks of a modern legal system. It also strives to achieve justice, promote freedom, and protect our security. This *Very Short Introduction* provides a clear, jargon-free account of modern legal systems, explaining how the law works both in the Western tradition and around the world.

www.oup.com/vsi

PHILOSOPHY OF LAW

A Very Short Introduction

SECOND EDITION

Raymond Wacks

The concept of law lies at the heart of our social and political life. Legal philosophy, or jurisprudence, explores the notion of law and its role in society, illuminating its meaning and its relation to the universal questions of justice, rights, and morality.

In this Very Short Introduction Raymond Wacks analyses the nature and purpose of the legal system, and the practice by courts, lawyers, and judges. Wacks reveals the intriguing and challenging nature of legal philosophy with clarity and enthusiasm, providing an enlightening guide to the central questions of legal theory.

In this revised edition Wacks makes a number of updates including new material on legal realism, changes to the approach to the analysis of law and legal theory, and updates to historical and anthropological jurisprudence.

www.oup.com/vsi

EUROPEAN UNION LAW

A Very Short Introduction

Anthony Arnull

The European Union is rarely out of the news and, as it deals with the consequences of the Brexit vote and struggles to emerge from the eurozone crisis, it faces difficult questions about its future. In this debate, the law has a central role to play, whether the issue be the governance of the eurozone, the internal market, 'clawing back powers from Europe' or reducing so-called 'Brussels red tape'.

In this *Very Short Introduction* Anthony Arnull looks at the laws and legal system of the European Union, including EU courts, and discusses the range of issues that the European Union has been given the power to regulate, such as the free movement of goods and people. He considers why an organisation based on international treaties has proved capable of having far-reaching effects on both its Member States and on countries that lie beyond its borders. Answering some of the key questions surrounding EU law, Arnull considers the future for the European Union.

www.oup.com/vsi